CANCÚN & THE YUCATÁN

ENCOUNTER

GREG BENCHWICK

Cancún & the Yucatán Encounter

Published by Lonely Planet Publications Pty Ltd
ABN 36 005 607 983

Australia (Head Office)	Locked Bag 1, Footscray, Vic 3011 ☎ 03 8379 8000 fax 03 8379 8111
USA	150 Linden St, Oakland, CA 94607 ☎ 510 250 6400 toll free 800 275 8555 fax 510 893 8572
UK	2nd fl, 186 City Rd London EC1V 2NT ☎ 020 7106 2100 fax 020 7106 2101
Contact	talk2us@lonelyplanet.com lonelyplanet.com/contact

This title was commissioned in Lonely Planet's US office and produced by: **Commissioning Editor** Catherine Craddock-Carrillo **Coordinating Editors** Robyn Loughnane, Charlotte Orr **Coordinating Cartographers** Hunor Csutoros, Julie Dodkins **Layout Designers** Wibowo Rusli, Frank Deim **Managing Editor** Bruce Evans **Senior Editors** Katie Lynch, Helen Christinis **Managing Cartographers** Alison Lyall, David Connolly **Cover Image Research** Naomi Parker **Internal Image Research** Sabrina Dalbesio **Managing Layout Designer** Indra Kilfoyle **Language Content** Annelies Mertens, Branislava Vladisavljevic **Thanks to** Heather Dickson, Lisa Knights

Cover photograph Wooden pier above a tropical lagoon in Cancún, Paolo Curto/Photolibrary.

Printed through Colorcraft Ltd, Hong Kong.
Printed in China.

HOW TO USE THIS BOOK

Color-Coding & Maps

Color-coding is used for symbols on maps and in the text that they relate to (eg all eating venues on the maps and in the text are given a green knife and fork symbol). Each beach and town also gets its own colour, and this is used down the edge of the page and throughout that beach and town section.

Shaded yellow areas on the maps denote areas of interest – for their historical significance, their attractive architecture or their great bars and restaurants. We encourage you to head to these areas and just start exploring!

Send us your feedback We love to hear from readers – your comments help make our books better. We read every word you send us, and we always guarantee that your feedback goes straight to the appropriate authors. The most useful submissions are rewarded with a free book. To send us your updates and find out about Lonely Planet events, newsletters and travel news visit our award-winning website: ***lonelyplanet.com***.

Note: We may edit, reproduce and incorporate your comments in Lonely Planet products such as guidebooks, websites and digital products, so let us know if you don't want your comments reproduced or your name acknowledged. For a copy of our privacy policy visit ***lonelyplanet.com/privacy***.

GREG BENCHWICK

Greg first visited the Yucatán Peninsula in the early '80s, when his old man took him and his sister to the tiny coastal village of Akumal. They snorkeled with barracuda and parrot fish in the Laguna Yal-Kú, took a nauseating ferry over to Cozumel and even visited the remote ruins of Cobá. While his present-day journeys will never compete with the rosy-hued memories of the past, Greg's been coming back ever since… though he swears the Nohoch Mul pyramid in Cobá has shrunk. Greg's work has been featured in *Condé Nast Traveller, National Geographic Traveler, Wild Blue Yonder* and in over a dozen guidebooks on Latin America, including Lonely Planet's *Cancún, Cozumel & the Yucatán*. To see videos and podcasts from Greg's adventures, check out his website www.soundtraveler.com.

GREG'S THANKS

An enduring thanks goes out to the people of Mexico, who make every journey 'down south' a pleasure. Big props also go out to the people who helped with my local-voice interviews, including Juan de la Rosa, Deborah Felixson, Guadalupe Quintana and Iñaki Iturbe. And, of course, thanks and never-ending love to the two most beautiful women in the world: my wife and my mother.

At play on the beach at Playa Norte (p58), Isla Mujeres

CONTENTS

>THIS IS CANCÚN & THE YUCATÁN

An area of remarkable diversity and eye-popping natural beauty, the Yucatán Peninsula – and its crowning resort developments in Cancún and the Riviera Maya – offers something for just about everyone in your crew.

For bacchanalians and beach lovers, there are the devilish nightclubs and angelic white sands of Cancún and Playa del Carmen. Divers and adventurers will salivate at the sight of the translucent waters and massive coral arrays of the Mesoamerican reef – the second-largest barrier reef in the world. For everybody else, there are lost Maya ruins to explore, hammocks to test, Coronas to drink, and long-forgotten beaches to discover.

At the heart of it all is Cancún. As Mexico's most-visited resort area (this little spit of sand and sun draws in well over four million visitors each year), Cancún is many things to many people. Some say it's the best beach destination on the planet, while others find the over-the-top development to be crass and tacky. Truth be told, Cancún is all this and a whole lot more.

But there's more on offer along this coast than just the resorts of Cancún and the Riviera Maya. Out in the waters of the Caribbean, you have spectacular beaches and world-class diving on Isla Mujeres and Cozumel.

Further south along the Quintana Roo (kin-*tah*-nah roh) coast, you have the Euro-chic lounges of Playa del Carmen, the laid-back rhythms and spectacular coastal ruin at Tulum, plus a handful of azure-blue cenotes (limestone sinkholes perfect for swimming or diving) and lost lagoons found near cozy beach towns like Akumal and Mahahual.

Around here, the past and present intermingle. You'll see it in the towering temples at archaeological sites like Chichén Itzá and Cobá, in the cobblestone streets of the colonial centers of Mérida and Valladolid, and in the villages and culture of southern Mexico's native people, the Maya.

Top left Maya people carrying religious banners from Convento de San Antonio de Padua (p114) **Top right** A Mexican woman in traditional dress (p143) **Bottom** La Parrilla (p49), one of Cancún's authentic Mexican restaurants

>HIGHLIGHTS

DAVID RYAN

Lazing around at Laguna Bacalar (p107)

>1 FROM THE DEEP-BLUE DEPTHS

GLIDING THROUGH THE CLEAREST WATER YOU'VE EVER SEEN

From the deep-blue depths rises the Mesoamerican reef, the second-largest barrier reef in the world, making the Caribbean coast a snorkeling and water-sports destination par excellence. But you don't need to head out on a boat to revel in the whirlwind of marine life that calls the reef home: several ocean-front lagoons and coastal reefs offer spectacular swimming and snorkeling just outside your door.

Isla Mujeres (p56) has several good coastal swimming spots. And while the Yunque Reef is free (and easily accessible), it might be worth your time investing in a day of snorkeling at the beach at Hotel Garrafón de Castilla (p60). There's some excellent diving here as well and you are likely to see sea turtles, rays and barracuda in the translucent water. Or, you can pony up for an excursion to neighboring Isla Holbox (p116) to swim with whale sharks. Gliding alongside these gentle giants is often a trip highlight.

Between Isla Mujeres and Cancún an underwater museum (p38) is being built that will feature a remarkable collection of statuary. The sculptures are accessible to divers and snorkelers alike, while landlubbers might want to hire a glass-bottom boat.

Then there are the endless opportunities just off the shore of Cozumel (pictured right, p78). There's a decent snorkeling beach just off the main pier or you can head over to Parque Chankanaab for clear-blue waters (with a smattering of tourist kitsch thrown in for good measure). South of Playa del Carmen in the cozy resort village of Akumal (p77), you'll find excellent snorkeling at the Laguna Yal-Kú.

For travelers with a bit more time on their hands, the shimmering aqua-green waters right off the beach from the Costa Maya town of Mahahual (p102) are not to be missed. Also near Mahahual is the massive Banco Chinchorro, a biosphere reserve where you can dive down to age-old shipwrecks or simply cruise along, checking out the topsy-turvy corals and darting schools of iridescent reef fish.

But your aquatic adventures need not end there. With the extensive barrier reef protecting this coast's shores, there's fun to be had on nearly every beach. Bring your snorkel, goggles and fins, and head out to see the remarkable water worlds lying just beneath the surface of the glimmering Caribbean seas.

LEE FOSTER

>2 HISTORY'S PAST

TRAVELING BACK IN TIME AT AWE-INSPIRING MAYA RUINS

Caught between the relentless beat of progress and the echoes of tradition, the Yucatán Peninsula stands at a crossroads. On one side you have the brawny, glitzy megaresorts of the Caribbean coast; on the other are the proud, steadfast traditions of the modern Maya and the remarkable temples and pyramids constructed by their ancestors in well-preserved archaeological sites such as Chichén Itzá, Cobá and Tulum.

The highlight of any cultural explorer's vacation is a day trip to Chichén Itzá (pictured below, p110). Named one of the 'New Seven Wonders of the World,' this site has towering pyramids and a handful of nearby cenotes worth visiting. But if you want to actually test your mettle and climb a pyramid, it makes sense to head down to Cobá (p96), where Indiana Jones–style adventure awaits. And while nearby Tulum's coastal ruin lacks the same historical significance, you can't beat the tawny sunrise views.

But Yucatán's pre-Colombian treasures don't stop there. Driving through the countryside, you'll notice hills where none should be. These are the remnants of Maya cities and religious centers that have simply been taken over by the jungle. Grab a guide and head out for a day to explore these seldom-seen vestiges of a history stretching back thousands of years.

ARIADNE VAN ZANDBERGEN

>3 STRUTTING YOUR STUFF

LOOKING GOOD ON PLAYA DEL CARMEN'S TONY QUINTA AV

Looking good is nearly as important as feeling good. And you'll want to bust out your classiest dress sandals and sarong as you cruise from boutique to boutique on Playa del Carmen's posh Quinta Av pedestrian mall (p66). While T-shirt and trinket shops have found their home here, there are also great galleries and boutiques for the inner 'conspicuous consumer' in all of us. Plus, come sunset, the strip lights up with chillaxed lounges, rooftop night clubs and plenty of live music.

After the sun rises, you'll want to wash away the dregs of 'last night's whatever' with an adrenaline-pumping dive into the cleansing waters of nearby cenotes (p71) like Cenote Azul or El Jardín del Edén, or simply while away the day on the honey-brown beach. For the adventurous, there's diving and parasailing, but it might be tough to leave your little beach *palapa* (thatched-roof, open-sided structure) on Mamita's Beach long enough to take on an adventure that requires more than applying suntan lotion, sipping on a mojito and taking in the sun and waves.

DENNIS JOHNSON

>4 COUSTEAU'S DREAMWORLD

FLOATING ALONG THE SANTA ROSA WALL IN THE PRISTINE WATERS NEAR COZUMEL

Cozumel – and its 65 surrounding reefs – is, without a doubt, one of the most popular diving destinations in the world. Once a pilgrimage site of the Maya, the island was all but abandoned until Jacques Cousteau came here in 1961 to film the amazing reefs found just offshore.

The island's waters are blessed with fantastic year-round visibility (commonly 100ft or more), and a jaw-droppingly impressive variety of marine life that includes spotted eagle rays, moray eels, groupers, barracudas, turtles, sharks, brain coral and some huge sponges. Whether you're a novice looking to head out on a first-time 'resort dive' or an old salt with hundreds of hours beneath your flippers, there's a dive here for you (p88).

The Santa Rosa Wall is the biggest of the famous sites. No matter where you're dropped, expect to sight parrot fish, grouper and barracuda, plus a Willy Wonka's worth of funky overhangs, tunnels, sponges and corals. The current is quick and you'll probably only get to check out a small portion of it on your first drift dive. Guess you'll need to come back...

Experts only need apply for a dive to the coral caverns of the Punta Sur reef. This large cave system features plenty of interesting corals, as well as your standard assortment of tropical fish.

Snorkelers and novices will love the placid waters in the Colombia Shallows and Palancar Gardens. The current is nice and calm, making it a good spot to just relax and float. And with maximum depths running between 30ft and 60ft, it's a good spot to get your feet wet (excuse the pun) or just take it easy on your ears.

Although Cozumel was hammered by two hurricanes (Emily and Wilma) in 2005, most of the island's diveable reefs, and all of the deeper ones, remained unharmed. Unsurprisingly, it was the snorkeling sites that were hardest hit; yet thanks to the tireless efforts of the local diving community (whose livelihood depends on the health of the reefs) and the natural resilience of this amazing ecosystem, things are returning to normal.

But Cozumel offers more than just diving. There are several small Maya sites found on this island, which once served as a pilgrimage spot for Maya women coming to worship the moon and fertility goddess Ixchel, not to mention plenty of open-air eateries waiting to refuel you before your next adventure.

CHRIS A CRUMLEY / ALAMY

>5 KIDS WILL BE KIDS

BEING A KID AT ONE OF THE AREA'S MANY ECOLOGICAL THEME PARKS

Heading down the highway from Cancún to Tulum, you're sure to pass nearly half a dozen environmentally themed 'green parks' (p69). And while these parks can be pricey the kids love it and you probably will too.

Just inland from Puerto Morelos, Selvatica Tours (p53) has a zip line and horseback tours. South of Puerto Morelos, the heavy artillery is pulled out at Xcaret (p69) and Xel-Há (pictured below, p69), where you can swim with dolphins, paddle through crystalline lagoons and catch a show featuring native dancing (but not the kind you'll see in any modern-day Maya village) all in one day.

More adventurous types will appreciate the all-terrain-vehicle tours and caving at Xplor (p69) and Aktunchen (p69). Alternatively, you can just head out into the countryside for a day, or down a lost beachfront dirt road (there's one just south of Tulum), and see what adventures kick up.

JOHN NEUBAUER

>6 INTO THE UNDERWORLD

DIVING PAST STALACTITES IN THE DEPTHS OF AN UNDERGROUND CENOTE

If you never descend into a limestone sinkhole for a cooling afternoon swim or a goose-bump-inducing cave dive, then you've only scratched the surface of this remarkably profound paradise.

The region is pocked by these massive underground water worlds. One of the best dives is had as you soar like an angel through the hydrogen sulfide fogs of Cenote Angelita (p92). Cenote Dos Ojos (p77), Gran Cenote (pictured below, p94) and Aktunchen (p69) round out the offering of excellent cave-diving opportunities.

For those who'd rather not descend into the dark with only a guide and a tank of oxygen as your lifeline, there's excellent swimming and snorkeling at the numerous cenotes just outside of Puerto Morelos (p52), Playa del Carmen (p71) and Tulum (p92). With a bit more time, you can extend your trip to take advantage of some of the region's most beautiful cenotes, found near the pastoral Yucatecan town of Cuzamá (p116).

DAVID PEEVERS

>7 HAVE TACO – WILL TRAVEL

LICKING YOUR FINGERS AFTER YOUR 10TH FISH TACO

The creation story of the Maya tells us that humans are made of corn, so it's only fitting that the region's major staple is, in fact, maize. They grind it for tortillas, put it in drinks and stews, and use it during ceremonies. They even offer it, with a bit of honey for good favor, to the *aluxes* (forest gnomes) that are said to roam the countryside. While much of the regional cuisine finds its base in other parts of Mexico – think tacos and enchiladas – Yucatán will always have its corn.

With so much coastline, there's bound to be some good fish here, too. Fry it, batter it, drench it in garlic or eat it raw in a delicate ceviche – no matter what your taste, you're certain to not be disappointed. *Tikin-xit* is a savory slow-cooked local favorite that's steamed in a banana leaf. And you'll definitely want to indulge in a crab or two – especially if you make it over to the Gulf coast.

Other regional faves include slow-stewed chicken or pork *pibil* (pictured right); wrapped in banana leaves and cooked underground for hours on end, this is the one must-try traditional dish. *Pavo en escabeche* (slow-cooked turkey, with a special local marinade known as a *recado* made from dry chilies, spices, herbs and vinegar) is also worth sampling, especially if you find yourself inland, as is a refreshing *sopa de lima* (lime soup).

Then, of course, there're plenty of little roadside stalls offering everything from fish tacos (you'll want to eat at least three) to out-of-sight – and possibly out-of-the-question – 'delicacies' like *menudo* (tripe) and *sesos* (brains). You'll also want to sample *panuchos* (a handmade tortilla stuffed with mashed black beans, fried till it puffs up, then topped with shredded turkey or chicken and thin slices of avocado and onion) and *salbutes* (*panucho* without the bean stuffing).

With all those spices, you'll definitely want to cleanse your palate and, lucky for you, there are tons of fresh fruit drinks on offer – have your waiter blend it with milk to make a refreshing *liquado* (basically a milk shake featuring the fruit of your choice) or excite your taste buds with a milky rice *horchata*. For the sweet tooth in your group, there is *arroz con leche* (rice pudding), flan or *queso napolitano* (a thicker version of the traditional flan), and *helados de agua* (water-based ice cream made with traditional fruits like papaya, mango, coconut and mamey).

Top your evening off with a fresh-made margarita, a perspiring *paloma* (tequila, grapefruit juice and a splash of soda), a *chelada* (beer on ice with lime and salt) or an ice-cold Dos Equis lager...better make that two – there's always time for one more in paradise.

GREG ELMS

>8 CULTURE ON EVERY CORNER

HEADING INLAND FOR UNIQUE GLIMPSES AT TRADITIONAL MAYA LIFE

While much of the Quintana Roo coast is dominated by tourism, one need only head inland – sometimes all it takes is stepping two blocks from the tourist zone in mainstream hubs like Cancún and Playa del Carmen – to catch fleeting glimpses of modern-day life in the Yucatán.

For the culturally curious, there're the cobblestone streets and museums found in the quaint center of colonial Mérida (the Catedral de San Ildefonso is pictured below, p115). Or you can take a day trip to nearby Valladolid (p111) – it's on the way to Chichén Itzá (p110) – or head out into the countryside to explore traditional Maya villages like Nuevo Durango (p94) and Tihosuco. No matter where you venture out of the tourist zones, you're bound to see an authentic snapshot of life that you would have otherwise missed.

SEAN CAFFREY

>9 FROM DUSK TILL DAWN

RELEASING YOUR ID AS YOU LIGHT UP THE NIGHT

Sure, exploring ruins and remote Maya villages is fun. But for many, a trip to Cancún or the Riviera Maya would not be complete without getting at least a little blotto at one of the coast's decadent nightclubs.

Cancún (p36) leads the way with large dance clubs, foam parties and plenty of spring-break high jinks. For fewer college students gone wild and more libertine beach lounges, you'll want to hit up the tranced-out lounges of Playa del Carmen (p66). By 1am, most everybody is at the beach dancing their asses off at the Blue Parrot Bar (p77) – might as well join them. And then there're the hundreds of small beachfront shacks and locals-only dives that'll keep your mojo flowing till sunrise.

CRIS HAIGH / ALAMY

>10 NATURAL TREASURES

SMELLING THE ROSES AT THE AREA'S BIOLOGICAL RESERVES

Despite ever-increasing development, the natural beauty of the chalkboard-flat Yucatán Peninsula abides. The ethereal coo of the motmot still reverberates overhead, while below writhe the insects and creepy-crawlies that keep this scrub-jungle land renewed year after year. And deep below, in the realm of Ah Puch (god of the underworld), gurgle freshwater rivers that pull their way through massive limestone caverns all the way to the pitch-perfect waters of the Caribbean and the gulf.

A natural adventure can begin basically right outside your door in the translucent waters of the Caribbean coast. There're marine reserves off Isla Mujeres, Cozumel, Isla Holbox and Mahahual. And inland, there're a few natural lagoons worth exploring, like the one at Punta Laguna (p94) and the Laguna Bacalar (p107). And while most folks choose to skip a jungle slog, it's worth looking into a kayak expedition through the mangrove waterways of the Sian Ka'an Biosphere Reserve (pictured below, p98) or a birding expedition from Isla Mujeres to the remote Isla Contoy (p64). True by-the-seat-of-their-pants types should consider extending their stay for a two- or three-day expedition to the Reserva de la Biosfera Calakmul (p118) or the bird-choked arteries of the Río Lagartos biosphere reserve (p112).

JOHN NEUBAUER

>CANCÚN & THE YUCATÁN CALENDAR

Cancún knows how to party, but there is much more to this region than guzzling tequila shots at the Coco Bongo. There are plenty of traditional festivals – both in Cancún and throughout the rest of the peninsula – that'll get your juices flowing. In addition to the major nationally celebrated festivals – like Carnaval, Semana Santa (Easter Week) and Día de la Independencia (Independence Day) – each town has its local saint's day, regional festivals and so on. Since much of this coast was uninhabited just 40 years ago, it's sometimes best to head inland for glimpses of traditional Yucatecan revelry. There's also a national public holiday just about every month, often the occasion for yet further merriment.

CARVER MOSTARDI / ALAMY

Fireworks celebrating Día de la Independencia (p24)

JANUARY

Día de los Reyes Magos

Held each January 6, Día de los Reyes Magos (Three Kings' Day or Epiphany) is the day when Mexican children traditionally receive gifts, rather than at Christmas (but some get two loads of presents).

FEBRUARY, MARCH & APRIL

Día de la Candelaría

Held on February 2, the religious celebration of Día de la Candelaría (Candlemas) commemorates the presentation of Jesus in the temple 40 days after his birth. It is celebrated with processions, bullfights and dancing in many towns.

Carnaval

A big bash preceding the 40-day penance of Lent, Carnaval takes place during the week or so before Ash Wednesday (which falls 46 days before Easter Sunday; late February or early March). It's festively celebrated throughout the peninsula – especially in Mérida, Cozumel and Chetumal – with parades, music, food, drink, dancing, fireworks and fun.

Semana Santa

Solemn processions move through the streets throughout Semana Santa (Holy Week), which starts on Palm Sunday (Domingo de Ramos). On Good Friday (Viernes Santo) there are dramatic reenactments of the passion play, with locals taking the role of penitents following their savior through the stations of the cross.

SUN WORSHIPPERS

While every major temple built by the Maya was constructed with the stars and planets in mind, modern-day sun worshippers can best appreciate the craftsmanship of these ancient astronomers by heading to either Chichén Itzá (p110) or Dzibilchaltún (just south of Mérida; p116) for the vernal or autumnal equinoxes (March 20 or 21 and September 22 or 23). At the massive Chichén Itzá celebration, a shadowy serpent appears on the side of the El Castillo pyramid; while at Dzibilchaltún, the sun aligns with the doorway of the Temple of the Seven Dolls.

SEPTEMBER

Día de la Independencia

Every year on September 16, Día de la Independencia (Independence Day), the anniversary of the start of Mexico's War of Independence in 1810, provokes an upsurge of patriotic feeling. On the evening of the 15th, the words of Padre Miguel Hidalgo's famous call to rebellion, the Grito de Dolores, are repeated from the balcony of every town hall in the land.

NOVEMBER

Día de Todos los Santos & Día de Muertos

On November 1 and 2, Día de Todos los Santos (All Saints' Day) and Día de Muertos (Day of the Dead) form one of Mexico's signature fiestas, when the souls of the dead are believed to return to earth. Families build altars in their homes and visit graveyards to commune with their dead, taking garlands and gifts. A happy atmosphere prevails.

Riviera Maya Jazz Festival

www.rivieramayajazzfestival.com

Playa del Carmen hosts this free series of jazz concerts in late November. Performers have included the likes of Herbie Hancock and Al Jarreau.

DECEMBER

Día de Nuestra Señora de Guadalupe

A week or more of celebrations throughout Mexico leads up to Día de Nuestra Señora de Guadalupe (Day of Our Lady of Guadalupe), venerating the Virgin Mary, who appeared to an indigenous Mexican, Juan Diego, in 1531, and has since become Mexico's religious patron. Boys are taken to church dressed as little Juan Diegos; girls, in traditional indigenous dress. Held on December 12.

A local Maya woman decorating a family tomb for the Día de Muertos

JEFFREY BECOM

Children performing in procession during Christmas celebrations DOUG MCKINLAY

Posadas

From December 16 to 24, nine nights of candlelit parades reenact the journey of Mary and Joseph to Bethlehem. This festival is more important in small towns than cities.

Día de Navidad

Día de Navidad (Christmas) is traditionally celebrated with a feast in the early hours of December 25, after midnight Mass.

>ITINERARIES

ERIC WHEATER

Increase your culture quotient at Chichén Itzá (p110)

Rainforest
CAFE
CoCo
BONGO
CoCo
BONGO

>ITINERARIES

There's a lot of coast out there and, whether you choose to stay in frenetic downtown Cancún, laid-back Tulum, sophisticated Playa del Carmen or in a big-time all-inclusive resort along the Riviera Maya, it's probably best to focus your excursions to specific activities or attractions – less travel, more play.

DAY ONE

Better move quick or you'll miss it. Start and end your day with some quality beach time. If you want to go snorkeling or diving, hire a boat the day before to take you out to the excellent offshore sites near Isla Mujeres (p59) and Cozumel (p80). Cultural explorers should consider a journey to Chichén Itzá (p110), with a stop at the nearby cenotes on the way back.

DAY TWO

On day two, you'll have more of the same, perhaps with an early morning shopping spree in Cancún's markets (p47), along Playa del Carmen's Quinta Av (p71) or at the excellent market in Puerto Morelos (p54), which is especially lively on Sundays. From there, rent a car and head to Tulum (p90) to check out the ruins. On the way back, you can stop for a cooling afternoon swim in Akumal's Laguna Yal-Kú (p77). Be sure to leave some fuel in the tank for sunset drinks at Playa's Fusion (p76) or high-octane fun at Cancún's Coco Bongo (p43).

DAY THREE

Shake off the cobwebs with a jolting dive into a nearby cenote: in Cancún try Siete Bocas (p53); Cristalino Cenote (p71) is perfect for Playa; while Gran Cenote (p94) is the sinkhole of choice from Tulum.

Then it's time to get a bit off the tourist track. From Tulum, try heading to the Maya ruins at Cobá (p96) or you can also cruise down for a day of kayaking in the Sian Ka'an Biosphere Reserve (p98). Those stationed in Cozumel might want to rent a bike and tour the island (p80). From the northern portions of the state (around Cancún and Playa), you might

Top left Discover quiet Valladolid (p111) **Top right** Dance the night away at Coco Bongo (p43) **Bottom** Dip into the water at Playa del Carmen (p66)

FORWARD PLANNING

Practically no advance planning is necessary for a fun trip to Cancún and the rest of this sizzling tropical coast. But, for those of you who pack your bags two months before the flight leaves, here's a few top tips to get you started.

Three to six months before you go Enroll in a Spanish class at your local university or take a PADI diving-certification course, so you'll be zooted and suited for diving in Cozumel (p80), ordering drinks in Cancún (p42) or extending your language skills at a school in Playa del Carmen (p68). You'll also want to book your room way ahead if you are planning on visiting in December or during US spring break. And make sure your passport is up to date.

Three months before you go Book your diving or snorkeling expeditions with a good shop in Playa del Carmen (p68) or Cozumel (p80) – you can normally just reserve space when you get there, but it's always good to think ahead. You'll also want to arrange whale-shark trips to Isla Holbox (p116) with a bit of advance notice. Those renting a house should have it booked by now; www.locogringo.com is a good source.

Two weeks before you go Your hotel should be booked, especially in Cancún and the Riviera Maya. You may also want to check out *Cancun Tips* (www.cancuntips.com.mx) and *Yucatán Today* (www.yucatantoday.com) to see which restaurants are hot and which are not. If you're considering a spa treatment at Aqua (p39) or day trips from Cancún (p43), now's the time to reserve your car, figure out schedules and arrange some adventures for the kids (p128).

want to hit up an ecopark (p69) if you have kids, or you could arrange an excursion to remote Isla Contoy (p64) or Isla Holbox (p116).

DIVING & SNORKELING

Divers and snorkelers must – yes, must – head to Cozumel. The Santa Rosa Wall (p88) is Cozumel's most famous dive – you'll only see one-third of the wall's amazing sights with one tank. Snorkelers and novice divers should head to the Colombia Shallows (p88) for great visibility and some of the area's most spectacular coral formations.

Then cross to the mainland for a cenote dive at Cenote Angelita (p92) or Cenote Dos Ojos (p77). With a little more time, you can cruise down to Costa Maya for trips out to Banco Chinchorro (p107).

CULTURAL EXPLORER

Start with a trip through the colonial city of Valladolid (p111) to the must-see Unesco World Heritage site of Chichén Itzá (p110). From there, journey on to the jungle-shrouded ruins at Cobá (p96), a fascinating site that rates high on the adventure scale, stopping for the night at the coastal Maya site at Tulum (p92).

History is a living, breathing thing on the Yucatán Peninsula and those interested in witnessing the rhythm of modern-day life should take time to travel through the Maya countryside, stopping in towns like Tihosuco and Izamal (p113), on their way to the modern-day cultural capital of the region, Mérida (p115).

BACCHANALIAN BRAWL

This place knows how to party. No matter where you are, there's almost always time to stop for an afternoon *cerveza* (beer) or two. From there, it's on to pumping nightclubs in Cancún's Zona Hotelera, like Coco Bongo (p43) and Dady'O (p44). Those seeking a bit of blue-note cool should check out Roots (p51) in downtown Cancún. The party in Playa starts in the uberchic lounges along Quinta Av (p76), moving down to the beachfront discos after midnight (p77). While Cozumel can be a real snoozefest, Isla Mujeres' scene (p64) is as cool and peaced out as it gets.

>BEACHES & TOWNS

JOHN NEUBAUER

Handicrafts for sale on a Cozumel beach (p78)

>BEACHES & TOWNS

You'd think that as one of Mexico's most visited states, it'd be impossible to find a bit of solitude in Quintana Roo. But beyond the thumping clubs of Cancún and crowded theme parks of the Riviera Maya, you just might find your own quiet sliver of paradise.

There are talcum-powder beaches stretching all the way from Cancún to the Belizean border, unassuming Caribbean islands protected by the world's second-largest barrier reef, and impressive Maya sites throughout this long, arching sliver of limestone, salt and sea.

It's the peninsula's superstate, highly developed, heavily touristed, easy to get around and chock-full of opportunities for adventure – from exploring the depths of the region's numerous cenotes (limestone sinkholes filled with fresh water) to beating your own path to the mysterious ruins at Cobá and Tulum. This Caribbean coast also offers the best diving and snorkeling in all of Mexico. And for the kids there're ecological theme parks and heart-racing zip-line rides.

Most trips to Quintana Roo (kin-*tah*-nah roh) will begin and end in Cancún. Sure, it's mainstream, but this resort town does have its upsides, namely large hotels loaded with creature comforts and one of the best stretches of sand and sun around. Chicer-than-thou Playa del Carmen brings in a European crowd with its limelight lounges and libertine beach scene. Cozumel attracts mostly divers and cruise-ship visitors, while Isla Mujeres stands out for its lo-fi, low-key attitude and glimmering white beaches.

Further down the coast, Tulum boasts an immaculately preserved Maya ruin, plus a laid-back vibe that'll have you extending your travel plans for at least another week. Continue your trip down from there and you'll find some of the Caribbean's best beaches – not to mention top-notch diving – along the remote Costa Maya. Wherever you end up, don't forget to stop at the traditional Maya villages, coastal hamlets and lost ruins that give this region its unique spirit and energy.

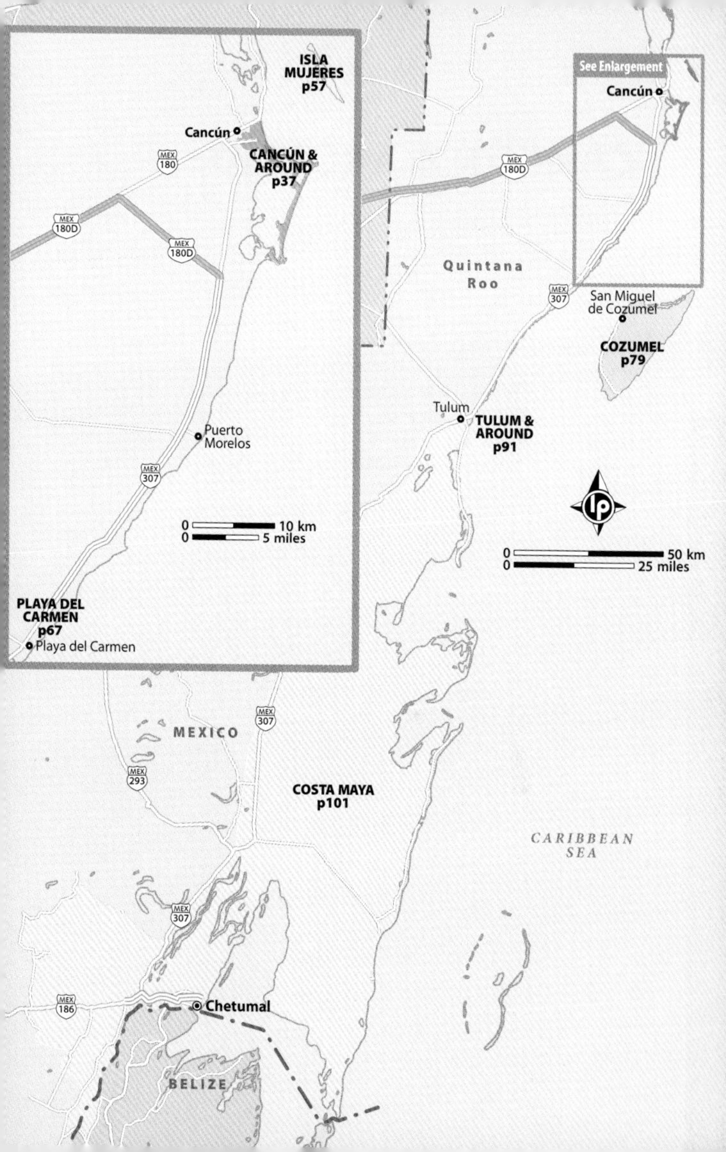

ISLA MUJERES p57
Cancún
CANCÚN & AROUND p37
MEX 180
MEX 180D
MEX 180D
Puerto Morelos
MEX 307
0 10 km
0 5 miles
PLAYA DEL CARMEN p67
Playa del Carmen
See Enlargement
Cancún
MEX 180D
Quintana Roo
MEX 307
San Miguel de Cozumel
COZUMEL p79
Tulum
TULUM & AROUND p91
0 50 km
0 25 miles
MEX 307
MEXICO
MEX 293
COSTA MAYA p101
CARIBBEAN SEA
MEX 307
MEX 186
Chetumal
BELIZE

>CANCÚN & AROUND

Unlike many cities in the world, Cancún just isn't afraid. It's unabashed and unapologetic, and therein lies its high-gloss charm. So send in the Maya dancers, swashbuckling pirates and beer-chugging US spring breakers. Cancún can take it. But can you?

Like Las Vegas, Ibiza or Dubai, Cancún is a party city that just won't give up. Top that off with a pretty damned good beach and you have one of the western hemisphere's biggest tourist draws, annually bringing in as many as four million visitors (mostly from the US). And with this many visitors you have crime and corruption, over-the-top, outrageously overhyped tourist traps, clamor and clutter. You also have a boomtown economic juggernaut and accidental metropolis with growing culinary sophistication. There are a few hip nightspots in the old downtown area and even some relatively authentic market areas.

Those seeking to escape the crowds might consider staying in nearby Puerto Morelos, a quaint beach town just 30 minutes down the road, or in one of the numerous all-inclusive resorts on the Riviera Maya.

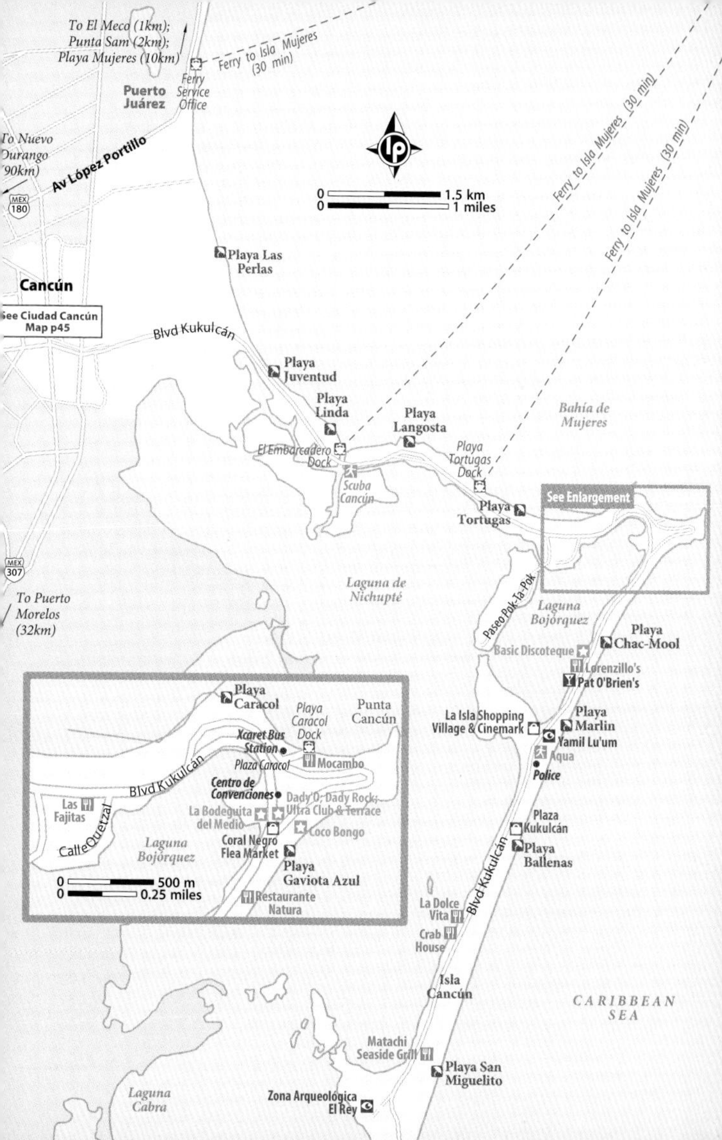

To El Meco (1km);
Punta Sam (2km);
Playa Mujeres (10km)
Ferry to Isla Mujeres (30 min)
Ferry Service Office
Puerto Juárez
To Nuevo Durango (90km)
Av López Portillo
MEX 180
0 1.5 km
0 1 miles
Ferry to Isla Mujeres (30 min)
Ferry to Isla Mujeres (30 min)
Playa Las Perlas
Cancún
See Ciudad Cancún Map p45
Blvd Kukulcán
Playa Juventud
Playa Linda
Playa Langosta
Bahía de Mujeres
El Embarcadero Dock
Scuba Cancún
Playa Tortugas Dock
Playa Tortugas
See Enlargement
MEX 307
To Puerto Morelos (32km)
Laguna de Nichupté
Paseo Pok-Ta-Pok
Laguna Bojórquez
Playa Chac-Mool
Basic Discoteque
Lorenzillo's
Pat O'Brien's
Playa Caracol
Playa Caracol Dock
Punta Cancún
Xcaret Bus Station
Plaza Caracol
Mocambo
Blvd Kukulcán
Centro de Convenciones
Dady'O; Dady Rock; Ultra Club & Terrace
Las Fajitas
La Bodeguita del Medio
Coco Bongo
Calle Quetzal
Laguna Bojórquez
Coral Negro Flea Market
Playa Gaviota Azul
0 500 m
0 0.25 miles
Restaurante Natura
La Isla Shopping Village & Cinemark
Playa Marlin
Yamil Lu'um
Aqua
Police
Plaza Kukulcán
Playa Ballenas
Blvd Kukulcán
La Dolce Vita
Crab House
Isla Cancún
CARIBBEAN SEA
Matachi Seaside Grill
Playa San Miguelito
Laguna Cabra
Zona Arqueológica El Rey

ZONA HOTELERA

The Zona Hotelera is what most people think of when they say 'Cancún': the sandy spit that encloses a scenic lagoon on one side and has the Caribbean's azure-greens on the other. This is where you'll find the best hotels, beaches and nightclubs.

SEE

CANCÚN UNDERWATER MUSEUM

☎ 998-848-83-12; www.asociadosnauticoscancun.com

This aquatic 'museum' had just three submerged sculptures at the start of 2010, but will eventually feature some 400 sculptures by Jason de Caires, submerged in the shallow waters between the Zona Hotelera and Isla Mujeres. While some of the sculptures will be accessible only by divers, you will be able to see many from glass-bottomed boats or with snorkel gear.

YAMIL LU'UM

admission free

Also known as the Templo de Alacran (Scorpion's Temple), this site was used between 1200 and 1500, and sits atop a beachside knoll in the parklike grounds between

REVEALING CANCÚN'S BRIEF HISTORY

When you look around at the giant hotels and supermalls, it's hard to imagine that pre-1970s there was nothing here but sand and a few fishermen. In the 1970s Mexico's ambitious planners decided to outdo Acapulco with a brand-new, world-class resort located on the Yucatán Peninsula. The place they chose was a deserted sand spit located offshore from the little fishing village of Puerto Juárez, on the peninsula's eastern shore: Cancún. Vast sums were sunk into landscaping and infrastructure, yielding straight, well-paved roads, potable tap water and great swaths of sandy beach.

Hurricanes Wilma and Emily whipped into town in 2005, destroying hotels in the area, flooding much of the city and carrying off tons of Cancún's precious beach sand. The hotels have been rebuilt and the government invested nearly M$200 million to restore the beaches – and it worked...at least for a while – but the sand is beginning to wash away again. So the government is planning on excavating 5.6 million cubic meters of sand from around Cozumel and Isla Mujeres at an estimated cost of around M$600 million to rebuild Cancún's beaches. Environmentalists have tried to file a lawsuit to stop the project – saying doing so will lead to massive environmental degradation – but a Mexican judge ruled that the environmentalists will need to post a M$15 million bond to file the case. While the environmentalists plan to appeal the ruling, this sum may put an end to any legal challenges.

ACCESSING THE BEACH

Under Mexican law you have the right to walk and swim on every beach in the country except those within military compounds. In practice it is difficult to approach many stretches of beach without walking through the lobby of a hotel, particularly in the Zona Hotelera. However, as long as you look like a tourist (this shouldn't be hard, right?), you'll usually be permitted to cross the lobby and proceed to the beach.

Starting from Ciudad Cancún in the northwest, all of Isla Cancún's beaches are on the left-hand side of the road (the lagoon is on your right). The first beaches are Playa Las Perlas, Playa Juventud, Playa Linda, Playa Langosta, Playa Tortugas and Playa Caracol; after you round Punta Cancún, the beaches to the south are Playa Gaviota Azul, Playa Chac-Mool, Playa Marlin, the long stretch of Playa Ballenas, Playa San Miguelito and finally, at Km 17, Playa Delfines. Delfines is about the only beach with a public parking lot big enough to be useful; unfortunately, its sand is coarser and darker than the exquisite fine, white sand of the more northerly beaches.

the Park Royal and The Westin. To reach the site, visitors must pass through either of the hotels flanking it or approach it from the beach (the easiest way).

ZONA ARQUEOLÓGICA EL REY

Blvd Kukulcán Km 17.5; admission M$39; 8am-5pm

There's a small temple and several ceremonial platforms at this rather unimpressive Maya site, but there are plans to build a museum here and it provides a good intro to better things to come in Chichén Itzá and Tulum.

DO

There's a good 17-plus miles of beach here. Playas Chac-Mool and Marlin can get a bit rough, making for good surf and bad swimming. Lifeguards normally post flags: blue (safe), red (unsafe), yellow (use precaution). For good diving and snorkeling, you'll need to take a boat.

AQUA *Spa*

998-881-76-00, ext 7620; www.spaaqua.com; Blvd Kukulcán Km 12.5

Call ahead to book your spa treatment at this large resort hotel. The spa is open to the public and comes complete with hot and cold whirlpool tubs, meditation zones and steam rooms. You can choose to enjoy your massage, facial or body treatment indoors or out. The hotel even has its own on-site tai chi master. Nice.

SCUBA CANCÚN *Water Sports*

☎ 998-849-52-26; www.scubacancun.com.mx; Blvd Kukulcán Km 5.2

This family-owned, PADI-certified operation was the first dive shop in Cancún. It offers a Cancún snorkeling tour for M$377 and a variety of dive options (including cenote, night and nitrox dives) at reasonable prices (one/two tanks cost M$702/884, equipment rental extra). It also arranges fishing trips.

VICTOR MARTINEZ *Water Sports*

☎ cell phone 998-1881404

Ever think of flying over the water at 40mph with a giant kite tied to your waste? Well, kiteboarding might just be for you. And the best way to get into this equipment-intensive sport is by taking a lesson.

SHOP

CORAL NEGRO FLEA MARKET *Artisanía*

Blvd Kukulcán Km 9.2

You'll get better deals – and better wares – at the markets in downtown Cancún or down south in Puerto Morelos, but it's fun stopping to try on the *lucha libre* (big-time wrestling) masks and maybe buy a bit of kitsch for your aunt.

LA ISLA SHOPPING VILLAGE *Mall*

Blvd Kukulcán Km 12

Unique among the island's malls, this is an indoor-outdoor place, with canals, an aquarium, ultramodern parasol structures and enough other visual distractions to keep even shopping-haters amused. Plus, you'll be able to buy souvenir T-shirts for the kiddos, overpriced silver for the wife (or husband) and plenty of IZOD polos for the suppressed yuppie in all of us.

PLAZA KUKULCÁN *Mall*

Blvd Kukulcán Km 13

The largest (and definitely among the stuffiest, attitude-wise) of the

Get lost in Plaza Kukulcán

DAVID PEEVERS

indoor malls is chichi Plaza Kukulcán. Of note here are the huge art gallery (taking up nearly half of the 2nd floor) and the many stores selling silverwork.

EAT

CRAB HOUSE

Seafood $$$

☎ 998-885-39-36; Blvd Kukulcán Km 14.8; 1-11:30pm

This gussied-up shack offers a lovely view of the lagoon that complements the seafood. The long menu includes many shrimp and fillet-of-fish dishes.

LA DOLCE VITA

Italian $$$

☎ 998-885-01-61; www.cancunitalianrestaurant.com; Blvd Kukulcán Km 14.6; noon-11pm

One of Cancún's fanciest Italian restaurants, it offers white wicker chairs and soft, romantic lighting, plus great lagoon views and attentive staff. Try the chicken with sun-dried tomatoes and finish with *crêpes Suzette* (for two).

LAS FAJITAS

Traditional Mexican $

Blvd Kukulcán Km 7.5; 7am-8pm Mon-Sat, to 5pm Sun

The best budget buy on this strip, this noisy roadside spot offers a complete breakfast for just M$30 and fresh mahimahi fillets for M$75 (they worked out a deal with a local diver to get fresh fish).

LORENZILLO'S

Seafood $$$

☎ 998-883-12-54; Blvd Kukulcán Km 10.5; 1pm-12:30am

Reputed by locals to be Cancún's best seafood restaurant, Lorenzillo's gives you 19 separate choices for your lobster presentation, including a taste-bud-popping chipotle, plum and tamarind

DON'T LEAVE HOME WITHOUT...

- Checking your foreign ministry's Mexico travel information.
- Clothes to cope with Yucatán's air-conditioned rooms (and buses) or the occasional cool, windy evening in *norte* (storm bringing wind and rain from the north) season.
- Any necessary immunizations or medications you require, including contraceptives.
- An inconspicuous container for money and valuables, such as a small, slim wallet or an under-the-clothes pouch or money belt.
- Your favorite sunglasses.
- A small padlock.
- A small Spanish dictionary and/or phrase book.
- Adequate travel insurance.
- Mosquito repellent.

sauce. Facing the lagoon, it's a good sunset joint.

MATACHI SEASIDE GRILL

Contemporary Mexican *$$$*

☎ 998-881-80-47; Blvd Kukulcán Km 17

The Matachi is a stylish, intimate place inside the Hilton, right on the beach. It offers Mexican- and Asian-inspired cuisine, including seafood, sushi and other creative dishes. Being one of the few seafront restaurants, it also has one of the best views in town.

MOCAMBO

Seafood *$$$*

☎ 998-883-03-98; Blvd Kukulcán Km 9.5

Definitely one of the best spots in the Zona Hotelera, the *palapa*-thatched Mocambo sits right on the ocean and serves up excellent seafood dishes, such as grouper, grilled conch and a savory seafood paella. There's live jazz here Tuesday through Sunday.

RESTAURANTE NATURA

Health Food *$$*

Blvd Kukulcán Km 9.8; V

Styled after the successful 100% Natural chain, this little bistro offers up a good mix of natural and vegetarian Mexican cuisine. Think giant natural juices and quesadillas with Chihuahua cheese, spinach, mushrooms and whole-wheat tortillas.

TAKING ON CANCÚN WITH KIDS

With such easy access to sand, sea and swimming pools, most kids will have a blast in Cancún. Some hotels offer babysitting or day-care services – be sure to check in advance if these are needed. Remember that the sun, strong enough to scald even the thickest of tourist hides, can be even more damaging for kids or babies: make sure your children are properly protected.

If the beach gets boring or you want a change of scene, check out the numerous **ecoparks** (p69) south of town. For a bit more culture, head over to the Maya ruins at **Chichén Itzá** (p110), **Tulum** (p90) or **Cobá** (p96).

DRINK

Often your hotel bar is the best spot to grab an afternoon drink.

PAT O'BRIEN'S *Bar*

Flamingo Mall, Blvd Kukulcán Km 11.5; noon-late

This is a good sunset cocktails place, despite the frat-boy vibe and sticky plastic glasses. Plus, we love the foosball table.

ULTRA CLUB & TERRACE

Lounge

Blvd Kukulcán Km 9; admission M$200-500; 10pm-dawn

Part of the Dady'O empire, this happening rooftop lounge gets going late and features a techno-heavy play list – a perfect spot to 'rage, rage against the dying of the light.' We think the late, great Dylan Thomas would approve.

PLAY

BASIC DISCOTEQUE *Dance Club*

Blvd Kukulcán Km 10.3; admission M$200-500; Fri-Sun 2am-dawn

Stay out late for two floors of sweaty, raunchy fun in this spaceship-looking outpost over the water. The musical selection tends toward electronica, but you'll get some salsa – and even some jazz – in there too.

CINEMARK *Cinema*

☎ 998-883-56-03; La Isla Shopping Village, Blvd Kukulcán Km 12; admission M$50

In general, Hollywood movies are shown in English with Spanish subtitles, although English-language children's movies are usually dubbed in Spanish.

COCO BONGO *Dance Club*

☎ 998-883-50-61; Forum Mall, Blvd Kukulcán Km 9; admission M$200-500; 10:30pm-5am

This is often the venue for MTV's coverage of spring break and tends to be a happening spot just about any day of the week. The club opens with celebrity impersonators,

DAY-TRIPPER: FIVE GREAT EXCURSIONS FROM CANCÚN

Go ahead, leave the all-inclusive for a day to check out the world beyond the little yellow wristband. And a quick sustainable travel tip: skip the group tour, using that extra dough to hire a local guide and buy some crafts.

Chichén Itzá (p110) Rent a car so you can take the old highway through Valladolid. Stop in the small Maya communities along the way for out-of-sight local fare.

Isla Mujeres (p56) Check out the turtle farm (see p58) in the morning, then swing up north to a sweet little swimming spot near the Avalon Reef Club (see p60).

Playa Mujeres and El Meco Just an eight-minute drive north of Punta Sam, you'll find this burgeoning tourist area. There are plans to build several resort-style hotels on Playa Mujeres. Currently, only the all-inclusive Excellence is up and running. On the way there, between Puerto Juárez and Punta Sam, you'll find El Meco, a small Maya site with just 14 structures.

Nuevo Durango and beyond Make your own way through the Maya hinterland as you explore the grassroots tourism efforts in small villages such as Nuevo Durango. Puerta Verde has more info on its website, www.puertaverde.com.mx.

Tulum (p90) Get up early and rent a car to make your way down to Tulum. Along the way, you'll want to stop at Akumal's Laguna Yal-Kú (p77) for a dip. On the way back, stop at one of the numerous cenotes clearly marked from the highway.

dancers and circus acts (clowns, acrobats and the like) for an hour or so, then the rock, pop and hip-hop start playing.

DADY ROCK *Live Music*

☎ 998-883-33-33; Blvd Kukulcán Km 9; admission free-M$200; 5:30pm-3:30am

A steamy rock-and-roll club (it plays techno on occasion) next door to Dady'O, Dady Rock attracts a slightly older crowd than its neighbor. Admission is free until 10pm.

DADY'O *Dance Club*

☎ 800-234-97-97; Blvd Kukulcán Km 9; admission M$200-500; 10pm-4:30am

Opposite the Forum Mall, the setting is a five-level black-walled faux cave with a two-level dance floor and what seem like zillions of laser beams and strobes. The predominant beats are Latin, house, techno, trance and hip-hop, and the crowd is mainly twentysomething.

LA BODEGUITA DEL MEDIO *Live Music*

Blvd Kukulcán Km 9; noon-late

One of our favorite chains in all of Mexico, this Cuban-themed bar has great live music, dancing and excellent mojitos. While it's fun for all ages, the older set will appreciate taking a break from the bump-and-grind scene at the other nightlife hot spots in the Zona Hotelera.

CIUDAD CANCÚN

Bustling, noisy and crowded, Ciudad Cancún is the place to find cheap eats and sleeps. There's

CIUDAD CANCÚN

DO

Armonizar T	1	C6
Koko Dog'z	2	D2
Nómadas Travel	3	C4
Teatro Xbalamqué	4	B3

SHOP

Chedraui Supermarket	5	C4
Fama	6	C3
Mercado 23	7	C1
Mercado 28	8	A3
Mercado Municipal Ki-Huic	9	C4

EAT

Carrillo's Lobster House	10	C3
Checándole	11	A3
El Tapatío	12	B2
Irori	13	C6
K Sadillas del Jalisco	14	D5
La Barbacoa de la Tulum	(see 24)	
La Habichuela	15	B3
La Parrilla	16	B2
La Res Cortés	17	B3
Los de Pescado	18	C5
Parque Las Palapas	19	C3
Restaurant 100% Natural	20	B3
Rolandi's Restaurant-Bar	21	C4
Ty-Coz	22	C2

DRINK

Karamba	23	C3
Plaza de Toros	24	D6

PLAY

Picante	25	C1
Roots	26	C3

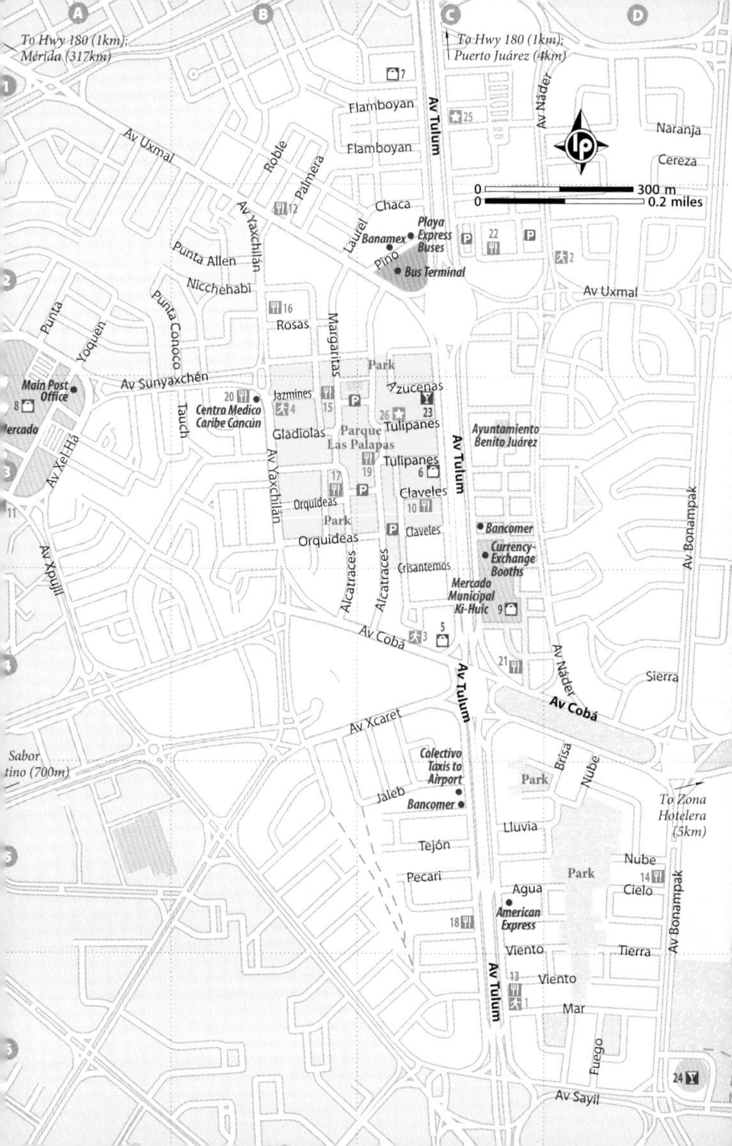

A
B
C
D
To Hwy 180 (1km); Mérida (317km)
To Hwy 180 (1km); Puerto Juárez (4km)
Flamboyan
Flamboyan
Av Tulum
Av Náder
Naranja
Cereza
0 300 m
0 0.2 miles
Av Uxmal
Roble
Palmera
Av Yaxchilán
Chaca
Laurel
Banamex
Playa Express Buses
Pino
Bus Terminal
Punta Allen
Nicchehabi
Punta Conoco
Av Uxmal
Punta
Yoquen
Rosas
Margaritas
Park
Azucenas
Main Post Office
Av Sunyaxchén
Centro Medico Caribe Cancún
Jazmines
Tauch
Gladiolas
Parque Las Palapas
Tulipanes
Tulipanes
Ayuntamiento Benito Juárez
ercado
Av Xel-Há
Av Yaxchilán
Orquideas
Park
Claveles
Claveles
Orquideas
Bancomer
Currency-Exchange Booths
Av Xpujil
Alcatraces
Alcatraces
Crisantemos
Mercado Municipal Ki-Huic
Av Bonampak
Av Cobá
Av Tulum
Av Náder
Sierra
Av Cobá
Av Xcaret
Sabor tino (700m)
Colectivo Taxis to Airport
Brisa
Nube
Park
Jaleb
Bancomer
To Zona Hotelera (5km)
Lluvia
Tejón
Nube
Pecari
Park
Cielo
Agua
American Express
Av Bonampak
Viento
Tierra
Av Tulum
Viento
Mar
Fuego
Av Sayil

also some good market areas and locals rule the clubs.

 DO

ARMONIZAR T *Courses*

cell phone 998-8982455; cnr Mar & Av Tulum

This downtown center offers yoga classes, holistic massage and dance therapy...but you can also get some quality dance therapy at the Coco Bongo (p43) in the Zona Hotelera.

KOKO DOG'Z *Water Sports*

www.kokodogz.com; Av Náder 41-42; noon-8pm Mon-Fri, to 6pm Sat

Cancún's only real surf shop sells all sorts of boards – surf, kite, body, skim – and arranges wakeboarding on the lagoon for M$1950 an hour per boat.

NÓMADAS TRAVEL *Tours*

998-892-23-20; www.nomadastravel.com; Av Cobá 5

This popular agency operates out of the lobby of Soberanis Hotel downtown, offering reasonably priced packages to popular destinations.

TEATRO XBALAMQUÉ *Courses*

998-887-38-28, ext 509; http://teatroxbalamque.blogspot.com; cnr Jazmines & Av Yaxchilán

Explore your inner artiste at this funky downtown learning center that offers yoga and theater courses. It's not SoHo, but it's the most boho scene Cancún has to offer.

> **THOSE MYSTERIOUS ALUXES**
>
> *Aluxes* (a-loosh-es) are Yucatecan forest sprites and many of the Maya still believe they can bring good or bad luck, even death, to those around them. Therefore, when forests are cleared, whether to make a field or build a house, offerings of food, alcohol and even cigarettes are made to placate them.

 SHOP

CHEDRAUI SUPERMARKET *Department Store*

Av Tulum

The upstairs clothing department here sometimes has souvenir-grade items at very affordable prices, plus you can stock up on picnic items for a road trip down the coast.

FAMA *Books*

998-884-65-41; Av Tulum 105 SM 22 M4 Lotes 27 & 27A

Magazines, atlases and books in several languages are the highlights of this store, located downtown near the southern section of Tulipanes.

MERCADO 23 *Market*

Av Tulum

If you're looking for a place *without* corny T-shirts, this is the place to go. There's a nice selection of masks and other artisan goods, probably crafted by hand in a nearby factory.

MERCADO 28 *Market*

Av Xel-Há

Head here to sample tacos at inexpensive food stalls. You can buy a hammer, a pair of shoes and a new T-shirt all within a few yards.

MERCADO MUNICIPAL KI-HUIC *Market*

Av Tulum

This warren of stalls and shops downtown carries a wide variety of souvenirs and handicrafts. It's better than the flea market in the Zona Hotelera, but not by much.

EAT

CARRILLO'S LOBSTER HOUSE *Seafood* $$$

998-884-12-27; Claveles 35

Try Carrillo's Plato Cozumel if you're looking for something a bit special. This somewhat formal restaurant has air-con indoors and is fan-cooled outdoors, and entertainment is provided by mariachis. Follow the good smells leading to the blue building.

Troll for bargains in Mercado 28 DAVID PEEVERS

CHECÁNDOLE

Traditional Mexican $$

998-884-71-47; Av Xpujil 6 SM 27; noon-8pm

If you can only eat at one restaurant in Ciudad Cancún, then you should eat here. Dressed up with a *palapa* roof, Checándole specializes in Chilango (Mexico City) cuisine. The *menú del día* (fixed three-course meal) is great value.

EL TAPATÍO

Traditional Mexican $

998-887-83-17; cnr Palmera & Av Uxmal; 9am-11:30pm

Touristy but good. A popular choice for hostelers, who suck

TRAVELING RESPONSIBLY

It's all about respect. Respect the locals, try to learn some of their language, respect the environment and its sanctity. And, above all, respect your mother!

Blue Flag (www.blueflag.org) An environmental accreditation program that focuses on marinas and beaches.

Caribbean Sustainable Tourism Alliance (www.cha-cast.com) Focuses mainly on the Caribbean, but also has some good reef ecology info.

Coral Reef Alliance (www.coral.org) Has reef protection guidelines.

Green Globe (www.greenglobe.org) For general information.

International Ecotourism Society (www.ecotourism.org) Lists ecofriendly businesses that have jumped through the hoops to gain accreditation.

Mexican Adventure & Ecotourism Association (www.amtave.org) Lists some of the region's ecotourism operators.

Mexiconservacion (www.mexiconservacion.org) Has a green guide to the Yucatán.

Puerta Verde (www.puertaverde.com.mx, in Spanish) Developing agritourism in Quintana Roo.

Responsibletravel.com (www.responsibletravel.com) For general information.

down the mammoth fruit and veggie juices, shakes and smoothies at any time of day, or dig into traditional Mexican fare.

IRORI *Japanese* $$$

☎ 998-892-30-72; Av Tulum 226; 1-11pm Mon-Sat, to 7pm Sun;

Enjoy the show as the chef slices and dices the night away at this Japanese-run restaurant. Sushi and many other Japanese favorites are served in an intimate and nicely decorated setting. There's even a kids' menu if you've got sushi-scoffing rug rats in tow.

K SADILLAS DEL JALISCO *Traditional Mexican* $

Av Bonampak 193; 8am-6pm Mon-Sat

For a cheap lunch on this side of town, head over to the *palapa*-shaded K Sadillas, where the friendly owner Javier serves up supercheap lunches, including – you guessed it – quesadillas.

LA BARBACOA DE LA TULUM *Traditional Mexican* $

Plaza de Toros, cnr Avs Bonampak & Sayil

Taco lovers shouldn't miss this down-home cantina. It's amazing that something so simple could be so difficult to do well, but the folks at La Barbacoa do it right.

LA HABICHUELA *Yucatecan* $$$

☎ 998-884-31-58; Margaritas 25

An elegant restaurant with a lovely courtyard dining area, La Habichuela offers up tremendous dishes such as shrimp and lobster in curry sauce served inside a coconut with tropical fruit, but almost anything on the menu is delicious.

LA PARRILLA

Traditional Mexican $$

☎ 998-884-81-93; Av Yaxchilán 51; ⏲ noon-2am

A traditional Mexican restaurant popular with locals and tourists alike, La Parrilla serves a varied menu, with dishes from all over Mexico, including Yucatecan specialties. If you're lucky, a waiter will serve you beer by balancing it on his head from the bar to your table.

LA RES CORTÉS

Traditional Mexican $

cnr Alcatraces & Orquideas; ⏲ 6pm-2am

This amazing little open-air restaurant looks right onto a park and serves up some of the city's best tacos, as well as other offerings

GETTING THERE & AROUND

Buses between downtown and the Zona Hotelera To reach the Zona Hotelera from Ciudad Cancún, catch any bus with 'R1,' 'Hoteles' or 'Zona Hotelera' displayed on the windshield as it travels along Av Tulum toward Av Cobá, then eastward on Av Cobá. The same bus returns from the Zona Hotelera into town. The one-way fare is M$7.50, but since change is often unavailable this varies between M$7 and M$8. Having correct change in advance makes things easier.

Puerto Juárez for Isla Mujeres ferries To reach Puerto Juárez' Isla Mujeres ferries, catch a Ruta 13 ('Pto Juárez' or 'Punta Sam'; M$7.50) bus heading north on Av Tulum. Some R1 buses make this trip as well; tickets cost M$8.50.

Taxis Cancún's taxis do not have meters. Fares are set, but you should always agree on a price before getting in, otherwise you could end up paying for a 'misunderstanding.' From Ciudad Cancún to Punta Cancún is M$80 to M$100, to Puerto Juárez M$30 to M$40. Within the Zona Hotelera or downtown zones costs around M$20 to M$40. Hourly and daily rates should run about M$150 to M$200 and M$700 to M$900 respectively.

Buses out of town Cancún's modern bus terminal occupies the wedge formed where Avs Uxmal and Tulum meet.

Minibuses to Playa del Carmen and Tulum Across Pino from the bus terminal, a few doors from Av Tulum, is the ticket office and miniterminal of Playa Express, which runs air-conditioned buses down the coast to Tulum approximately every half-hour until early evening, stopping at major towns and points of interest along the way.

Ticketbus (☎ 800-702-80-00; www.ticketbus.com.mx) An excellent online source for up-to-date bus schedules. See p146 for more details on buses, flights and boats leaving from Cancún.

ADO (☎ 800-802-80-00; www.ado.com.mx) The main first-class bus line in Quintana Roo, ADO has a ticket booth in the airport (just after you pass customs), where you can buy cheap tickets to downtown Cancún (M$42) and Playa del Carmen (M$106).

Try croissants at Ty-Coz

DAVID PEEVERS

reminiscent of the street fare in Guadalajara.

LOS DE PESCADO

Traditional Mexican $

Av Tulum 32; 10am-5:30pm

It's easy to order at this restaurant as there are only two choices: ceviche or tacos. Knock either back with a beer or two and you'll see why this is one of the best budget spots in Ciudad Cancún.

PARQUE LAS PALAPAS

Traditional Mexican $

Parque Las Palapas

Hang out with locals as you chow down on savory tacos and *tortas* (Mexican sandwiches) at any of this park's numerous food stalls. The busier the stall, the more likely it'll be clean.

RESTAURANT 100% NATURAL *Health Food* $$

Cien Por Ciento Natural; ☎ 998-884-01-02; Av Sunyaxchén; 7am-11pm; V

Vegetarians and health-food nuts delight at this health-food chain, which serves juice blends, a wide selection of yogurt-fruit-vegetable combinations, and brown rice, pasta, fish and chicken dishes.

ROLANDI'S RESTAURANT-BAR *Italian* $$

☎ 998-884-40-40; Av Cobá 12; 1pm-12:30am

A Swiss-Italian eatery with a wood-fired pizza oven, located between

Avs Tulum and Náder just off the southern traffic circle, Rolandi's serves elaborate pizzas, spaghetti plates and a range of northern Italian dishes.

TY-COZ *Bakery* $

☎ 998-884-60-60; Av Tulum; 9am-11pm Mon-Sat

This bakery has granite tabletops and a pleasing ambience, and serves good coffee, baguettes and croissants, as well as sandwiches made with a variety of meats and cheeses.

DRINK

Stroll along Av Yaxchilán down to Parque Las Palapas and you are sure to run into something (or somebody) you like.

KARAMBA *GLBT Bar*

☎ 998-884-00-32; cnr Azucenas & Av Tulum; admission free-M$100; 10pm-6am Thu-Sun

A venerable standby on the 2nd floor, this bar has frequent drink specials. Come here for a varied crowd of gays, lesbians and cross-dressers.

PLAZA DE TOROS *Cantina*

Bullring; cnr Avs Bonampak & Sayil

There are several bars, some with music, that draw a largely local crowd. And, no, you don't have to watch a bull get killed.

PLAY

PICANTE *GLBT Entertainment*

Av Tulum 20; 9pm-6am

This place isn't as 'spicy' as its name suggests, but it is a longtime neighborhood gay bar. It often features movies shown at high volume until about 1am, when the dance music comes on.

ROOTS *Live Music*

☎ 998-884-24-37; Tulipanes 26; admission Fri & Sat M$50; 6pm-1am Mon-Sat

Pretty much the hippest bar in Ciudad Cancún, Roots features jazz, reggae, rock bands and the occasional flamenco guitarist. The food here is good, too.

Check out Roots for blue-note cool DAVID PEEVERS

YUCATÁN FAST FACTS

Naming rights Legend has it that the peninsula got its name when the Spanish conquistadors asked the natives what they called their land. The response was *'yucatán'* – Maya for 'we don't understand you.'

Scariest number of the past thousand years More than 66.5 million Native Americans died within 150 years of the arrival of Columbus, according to some estimates.

Scariest date of the next thousand years On December 23, 2012, the Maya Long Count calendar reaches completion, signaling the end of our current universe, according to Maya cosmology.

SABOR LATINO *Dance Club*

☎ 998-892-19-16; cnr Avs Xcaret & Tankah; admission M$40-60; 🕐 10:30pm-6am, closed Sun-Tue low season

Located on the 2nd floor of Chinatown Plaza, this is a happening club. Live acts feature Dominican salsa and other tropical styles.

PUERTO MORELOS

Halfway between Cancún and Playa del Carmen, Puerto Morelos retains its quiet, small-town feel. While the village offers enough restaurants and bars to keep you entertained by night, it's really the shallow Caribbean waters that draw visitors here. Brilliantly contrasted stripes of bright green and dark blue separate the shore from the barrier reef – a tantalizing sight for divers and snorkelers – while inland a series of excellent cenotes beckon the adventurous.

SEE

JARDÍN BOTÁNICO YAAX CHE

admission M$70; 🕐 9am-5pm Mon-Sat

This 60-hectare nature reserve, located a mile south of the turnoff to Puerto Morelos, has around a mile and a half of trails through several native habitats. The preserve also holds a large animal population, including the only coastal troops of spider monkeys left in the region. For the anthropologically minded, the preserve has re-creations of a Maya house, as well as some genuine Maya ruins (c AD 1400). Bring insect repellent.

DO

BOCA DEL PUMA *Ecopark*

☎ 998-241-28-55; www.bocadelpuma.com;

Great for the kids, Boca del Puma offers a tour that takes you on five zip-line rides, followed by a dip in one of their cenotes. Located 10 miles west of Puerto Morelos.

DIVE PUERTO MORELOS *Water Sports*

☎ 998-206-90-84; www.divepuertomorelos.com; 8am-7pm

The barrier reef that runs along most of the coast of Quintana Roo is only half a mile offshore here, providing both divers and snorkelers with views of sea turtles, sharks, stingrays, eagle rays, moray eels and loads of colorful tropical fish. Several sunken ships make for great wreck diving, or you can arrange for a cenote dive. You'll also find dive shops in Hotel Ojo de Agua and Hotel del Cid.

GOYO'S *Tours*

☎ 998-221-26-79; adult/child under 12 years M$400/200

Goyo Morgan offers jungle tours. He can be difficult to locate at times, but is a wealth of information about the area, especially its edible and medicinal jungle plants. He also offers temascal (pre-Hispanic steam bath) sessions.

SELVATICA TOURS *Tours*

☎ 998-898-43-12; www.selvatica.com.mx; canopy tour adult/child 5-12yr M$1170/910; 7am-2pm

Inland from Puerto Morelos, this adventure outfit only runs prearranged tours. Come for adrenaline-pumping zip-lining, horseback rides and more. Canopy tour prices include transfer from Cancún-area hotels.

SIETE BOCAS *Ecopark*

admission M$60;

Located 8 miles west of Puerto Morelos, this lovely cenote has seven mouths – hence the name. For a bit extra, you can take a traditional temascal.

SNORKELING *Water Sports*

Puerto Morelos Dock

While the proximity of the reef makes it a tempting destination for beach-based swimmers, strong currents and lots of boat traffic can be hazardous. You're best off hiring a boat from the dock (M$300) or arranging to tag along with a dive-center group as they head out.

WILLOW STREAM *Spa*

☎ 984-206-30-38; www.willowstream.com; Fairmont Mayakoba Hotel, Carretera Federal Cancún–Playa del Carmen Km 298; 6:30am-9pm

Those in the know are calling this rambling 3700-sq-ft pleasure palace the best spa in all of Quintana Roo. And who's to argue? With treatments ranging from 75-minute massages to the two-person 'Alimento de los Dioses' treatment – which includes plenty of chocolate and your own private Jacuzzi – you just don't get much better than this. Advanced reservations required.

SHOP

ALMA LIBRE *Books*

☎ 998-871-07-13; www.almalibrebooks.com; 10am-3pm & 6-9pm Tue-Sat, 4-9pm Sun, closed Jul-Sep

This spot right on the plaza has more than 20,000 new and used books. The friendly owners are also a great resource for information about the area.

ARTISANS MARKET *Market*

One of the best reasons to come to Puerto Morelos is to hit the artisans market, a block south of the plaza's west corner, where you can find authentic Tixkokob hammocks, fine jewelry, pottery and clothing at much better prices than you'll see in Playa del Carmen or Cancún.

EAT

HOLA ASIA *Asian* $$

☎ 998-871-06-79; 1-10pm Wed-Mon

Once a tiny cafe, this local institution on the south side of the plaza has expanded yearly and now serves Japanese, Thai, Chinese and Indian dishes. General Tso's chicken and whole Thai fish are favorites. There's a bar and large dining area upstairs.

JOHN GRAY'S KITCHEN *Contemporary* $$$

☎ 998-871-06-65; Av Niños Héroes L6; 6-10pm Mon-Sat

One block west and two blocks north of the plaza, this 'kitchen' turns out some truly fabulous food. John, the personable owner-chef, has won international acclaim. The eclectic menu changes frequently.

LE CAFÉ D'AMANCIA *Cafe* $

8am-3pm & 6-10pm; V

This spotless place in the southwest corner of the plaza serves bagels, sandwiches, pies, coffee, and fruit and veggie *licuados* (milkshakes and blended drinks). There are internet machines (formerly known as computers) upstairs.

MAMA'S BAKERY *Bakery* $

☎ 998-845-68-10; Gomez s/n; 7:30am-2pm

At Mama's try the kiwi-raisin muffins, great carrot cake or the signature sticky buns. Yum! It also offers egg dishes and wonderful smoothies. This intimate, friendly place is a bit hard to find, so ask around.

TÍO'S *Traditional Mexican* $

6am-11pm

This local's joint across from the lighthouse serves great fish tacos in the morning and good Yucatecan dishes the rest of the time. Try the *panuchos* (tortilla stuffed with mashed beans, then fried and finally topped with shredded turkey or chicken, onion and slices of avocado).

DRINK

Puerto Morelos' nightlife scene is pretty chill. You can hop in a taxi or bus for a night of raunchy fun in neighboring Playa del Carmen or Cancún if you just can't stand the quiet.

BARA, BARA & QUE HORA ES *Bar*

noon-1am

These bookend bars next to Posada Amor are popular with the expat set. Que Hora Es draws in a younger crowd, while Bara, Bara works the 'Wastin' Away Again in Margaritaville' set.

DON PEPE'S *Karaoke Bar*

998-871-06-13; noon-3am

This is an old standby, popular with the mellow set and karaoke masters. Come here to hang out, talk, watch the plaza or catch live music if it happens to be on.

>ISLA MUJERES

If you are going to visit just one of Quintana Roo's islands, then Isla Mujeres (Island of Women) is probably the place for you. It's not as crowded as Cozumel, yet offers more to do and see than in relaxed and sleepy Holbox. Sure, there are quite a few ticky-tacky tourist shops, but folks still get around by golf cart and the crushed-coral beaches are better than those of Cozumel or Holbox.

The little island lies just northeast of Cancún and is an ideal day trip or a destination in its own right. There's not much here and that's the whole point: come to bask in quiet shallows or stretch out on the sand, snorkel or scuba dive, or just put on sunglasses and open that book you've been dying to finish. Come sunset, there're plenty of tasty options for your dinner and the nightlife scene moves at a good clip.

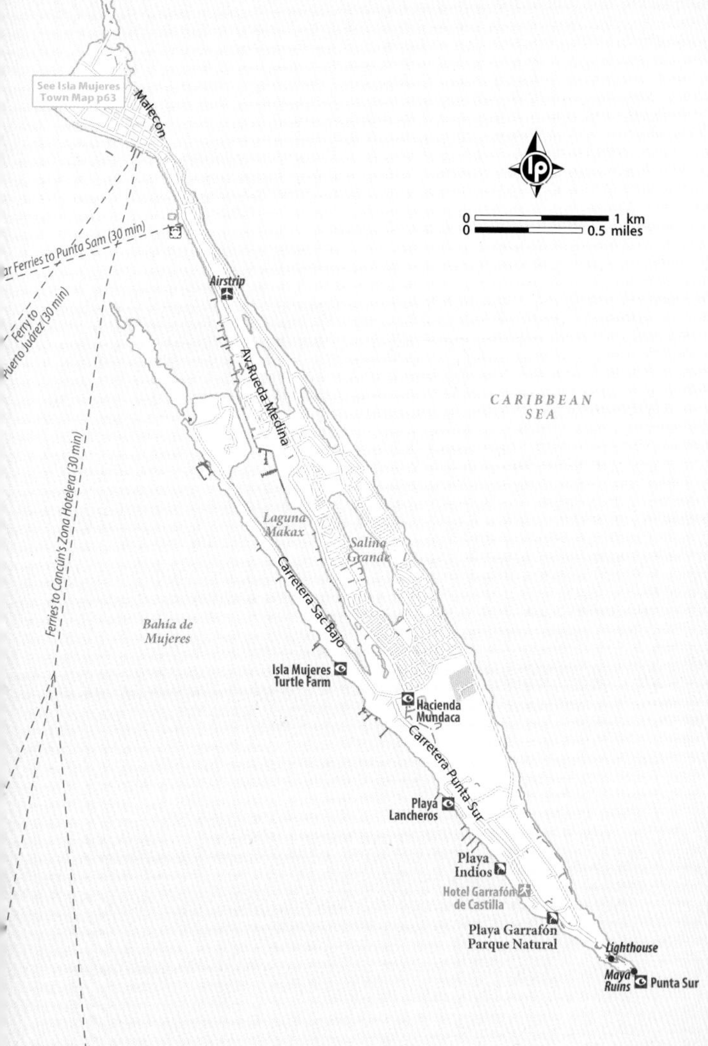

See Isla Mujeres Town Map p63
Malecón
0 1 km
0 0.5 miles
Car Ferries to Punta Sam (30 min)
Airstrip
Ferry to Puerto Juárez (30 min)
Av Rueda Medina
CARIBBEAN SEA
Ferries to Cancún's Zona Hotelera (30 min)
Laguna Makax
Salina Grande
Carretera Sac Bajo
Bahía de Mujeres
Isla Mujeres Turtle Farm
Hacienda Mundaca
Carretera Punta Sur
Playa Lancheros
Playa Indios
Hotel Garrafón de Castilla
Playa Garrafón Parque Natural
Lighthouse
Maya Ruins
Punta Sur

SEE

HACIENDA MUNDACA

Av Rueda Medina; admission M$13; 9am-5pm

Located about 2.5 miles south of the town, this ruined hacienda has shady grounds that make for pleasant strolling (bring insect repellent). There's a small zoo here. See opposite for more on the romantic history of the hacienda.

ISLA MUJERES TURTLE FARM

Isla Mujeres Tortugranja; 998-888-07-05; Carretera Sac Bajo Km 5; admission M$30; 9am-5pm;

In the 1980s, efforts by a local fisherman led to the founding of this hatchery and preserve, which protects the turtles' breeding grounds and places wire cages around their eggs to protect against predators.

PLAYA LANCHEROS

Located 3 miles south of town, the beach is less attractive than Playa Norte, but it sometimes has free musical festivities on Sundays.

Peacock-green water near Playa Norte DAVID PEEVERS

PLAYA NORTE

Once you see the island's main beach on its northern tip, you won't want to leave. Its warm

GETTING THERE & AROUND

Passenger ferries from Cancún Ferries depart from Puerto Juárez (one way M$35; take the R13 bus to get there from downtown Cancún for M$7.50) and the Zona Hotelera (one way M$135; terminals are located at Playa Linda and Playa Tortugas). The trip takes about 30 minutes and drops you right in downtown Isla Mujeres.

Getting around the island Many people find golf carts a good way to get around the island and caravans of them can be seen tooling down the roads. They average M$200 per hour and M$500 all day (9am to 5pm).

Pepe's Moto Rent (998-877-00-19) A good, no-nonsense place for both bikes and golf carts on Hidalgo between Matamoros and Abasolo.

UNREQUITED LOVE AT THE HACIENDA MUNDACA

The story of the Hacienda Mundaca is without a doubt much more intriguing than the ruins that remain. Fermín Antonio Mundaca de Marechaja, a 19th-century slave trader and reputed pirate, fell in love with a local woman known as La Trigueña (The Brunette). To win her, Mundaca built a two-story mansion complete with gardens and graceful archways, as well as a small fortification.

But while Mundaca was building the house, La Trigueña married another islander. Brokenhearted, Mundaca died and his house, fortress and garden fell into disrepair. Some documents indicate that Mundaca died during a visit to Mérida and was buried there. Others say he died on the island, and indeed there's a grave in the town cemetery that supposedly contains his remains. Despite the skull and crossbones on his headstone (a common *memento mori*), there's no evidence in history books that Mundaca was ever a pirate. Instead, it is said he accumulated his wealth by transporting slaves from Africa to Cuba, where they were forced to work in mines and sugarcane fields.

Today the mostly ruined complex has some walls and foundations, a large central pond, some rusting cannons and a partially rebuilt house. At the southern end stand a gateway and a small garden. You can still make out the words *Entrada de La Trigueña* (La Trigueña's Entrance) etched into the impressive stone arch of the gate.

shallow waters are the color of the greenest greens and bluest blues of a peacock feather and the beach is crushed coral.

PUNTA SUR

At the south end of the island you'll find a romantic lighthouse and the severely worn remains of a Maya temple dedicated to Ixchel. Unless you're desperate to pay the steep entry fee (M$50), head left before the lighthouse and enjoy the view from the small dirt parking lot.

DO

FELIPEZ WATER SPORTS CENTER *Water Sports*

☎ cell phone 998-2139544; felizpezfly fishing@yahoo.com.mx; Playa Norte

This operation on the beach at Playa Norte rents out kayaks (M$250 per hour) and sailboats (M$350 per hour). It also arranges fishing trips.

FISHERMAN'S COOPERATIVE BOOTH

Water Sports

☎ 998-877-13-63; Av Rueda Medina; snorkeling/fishing/Contoy/Holbox per trip M$260/1500/715/1250

The local fishermen have gotten together to offer trips to good snorkeling spots. Or you can take an entire day to visit the birds at Isla Contoy or the whale sharks of Isla Holbox (July through September).

HOTEL GARRAFÓN DE CASTILLA *Water Sports*

☎ 998-877-01-07; Carretera Punta Sur Km 6; admission M$30; 9am-5pm

A mile south of Lancheros you'll find this lovely swimming area. Avoid the overhyped and over-priced Parque Natural, using the hotel's facilities instead.

MUNDACA DIVERS *Water Sports*

☎ 998-999-20-71; mundacadivers@gmail.com; Madero 10; 1-tank dive/2-tank dive/snorkeling trip M$585/780/325

Within a short boat ride of the island there's a handful of lovely dives, such as **Barracuda**, **La Bandera**, **El Jigueo**, **El Frio** and **Manchones**. You can expect to see sea turtles, rays and barracuda, along with a wide array of hard and soft corals.

YUCATÁN FAST FACTS

Oh sweet relief The elite of the Classic Maya often received enemas of a sweet mead named *balché*. They also thought being cross-eyed was particularly beautiful.

Cross yourself twice Crosses adorned with *huipiles* (woven tunics) are found throughout the peninsula and are often associated with the cult of the speaking cross, which got its start in the peninsula's War of the Castes.

Quick reference Mexico Online (www.mexonline.com) has good history and culture links, plus lots of other information.

SEA HAWK DIVERS *Water Sports*

☎ 998-877-12-33; seahawkdivers@hotmail.com; Carlos Lazo

This time-honored dive and snorkel outfit has PADI courses and fishing trips. If you haven't been certified yet, this is one of the better spots on the island to do it.

SNORKELING *Water Sports*

The lagoon separating the Avalon Reef Club from the rest of the island (Yunque Reef) has a great shallow swimming spot. There's also good shore snorkeling near the Hotel Garrafón de Castilla and along the Malecón (look for sandy spots surrounded by reef). As always, watch for boat traffic when you head out snorkeling.

TOURIST INFORMATION OFFICE *Tours*

☎ 998-877-07-67; Av Rueda Medina; 8am-8pm Mon-Fri, 9am-2pm Sat & Sun

There's no sign, but the office is located between Madero and Morelos next to the Migracíones office. It offers a number of brochures and one member of its friendly staff speaks English; the rest speak Spanish only.

SHOP

Cruise the pedestrian mall on Hidalgo for handicrafts.

HOW THE ISLAND GOT ITS NAME

A glimpse at the sunbathers on the beach will have you thinking the moniker 'Island of Women' comes from the bikini-clad tourists. However, the name Isla Mujeres goes at least as far back as Spanish buccaneers, who (legend has it) kept their lovers in safe seclusion here while they plundered galleons and pillaged ports on the mainland. An alternate theory suggests that in 1517, when Francisco Hernández de Córdoba sailed from Cuba and arrived here to procure slaves, the expedition discovered a stone temple containing clay figurines of Maya goddesses; it is thought Córdoba named the island after the icons.

Today some archaeologists believe that the island was a stopover for the Maya en route to worship their goddess of the moon and fertility, Ixchel, on Cozumel. The clay idols are thought to have represented the goddess. The island may also have figured in the extensive Maya salt trade, which extended for hundreds of miles along the coastline.

MAÑANA *Books*

☎ 998-866-43-47; cnr Matamoros & Guerrero; 🕑 10am-7pm

This cafe has a nice selection of books, and swaps or sells, depending on your needs, though the selection tends to the 'Fabio on a white horse' end of the literary spectrum.

EAT

ALUXES COFFEE HOUSE

Cafe $

Matamoros; 🕑 8am-10pm Wed-Mon

Aluxes serves bagels with cream cheese, sandwiches, muffins, and hot and iced coffee (the perfect start to a day in sunned-and-salty Isla Mujeres).

LA LOMITA

Traditional Mexican $$

Juárez; 🕑 9am-10:30pm Mon-Sat

'The Little Hill' serves good, affordable Mexican food in a small, colorful setting. Seafood and chicken dishes predominate. Try the fantastic bean and avocado soup, or the ceviche.

MAÑANA *Cafe* $

☎ 998-877-05-55; cnr Matamoros & Guerrero; 🕑 8am-4pm; V

A good-vibe place with colorful hand-painted tables, superfriendly service and some excellent veggie options – the hummus and veggie baguette is the restaurant's signature dish – Mañana is perhaps the best lunch spot on the island.

MERCADO MUNICIPAL

Traditional Mexican $

Town Market; Guerrero

Inside the remodeled market are a couple of stalls selling cheap hot food. Other stalls sell a variety of produce, and a juice stand serves up liquid refreshments. Four open-air restaurants out the front serve simple, filling meals at fair prices.

MININOS *Seafood* $$

Av Rueda Medina; 11am-9pm

A tiny, colorfully painted shack with a sand floor right on the water, Mininos dishes up cocktails of shrimp, conch and octopus, as well as heaping plates of delicious ceviche and seafood soups.

PALETERÍA Y NEVERÍA LA MICHOACANA *Ice-Cream Parlor* $

cnr Hidalgo & Bravo; 9am-9pm

Near the plaza, this is the place to go for excellent, cheap milk shakes, fruit drinks and shaved ice.

PIZZA ROLANDI *Italian* $$

998-877-04-30; Hidalgo; 8am-11pm

This local chain bakes very good thin-crust pizzas and calzones in a wood-fired oven. The menu also includes pasta, fresh salads, fish, good coffee and some Italian specialties – definitely *don't* come here looking for Mexican.

RESTAURANTE BUCANEROS *Traditional Mexican* $$

998-877-02-10; Hidalgo; 7am-11pm

The best deal at this mostly outdoor restaurant is the *menú especial* (set menu), which gives you a choice of several mains accompanied by soup or salad and a dessert.

SATAY *Asian* $$$

998-848-84-84; López Mateos

Mix things up a little with the Thai red snapper or toro-and-papaya salad at this Asian fusion restaurant. It's not beachfront, but the modern, cool ambience is pleasant enough.

ISLA MUJERES TOWN

SEE
Playa Norte 1 A3

DO
Felipez Water Sports Center 2 A3
Fisherman's Cooperative Booth 3 C5
Mundaca Divers 4 C4
Sea Hawk Divers 5 B3
Tourist Information Office 6 C5

SHOP
Mañana .... (see 9)

EAT
Aluxes Coffee House 7 C4
La Lomita 8 D5
Mañana 9 C4
Mercado Municipal 10 B4
Mininos 11 B5
Paletería y Nevería La Michoacana 12 D5
Pizza Rolandi 13 C4
Restaurante Bucaneros 14 C4
Satay 15 A4
Sunset Grill 16 A4
Viva Cuba Libre 17 B4
Xpress Super 18 C4

DRINK
El Patio 19 C4
Playa Sol 20 A4
Poc-Na Hostel 21 C4

PLAY
Fayne's 22 B4
Hotel Na Balam 23 B2
La Luna 24 D4

A
B
C
D
1
2
3
4
5
6
Punta Norte
0
200 m
0
0.1 miles
Avalon Reef Club
Yunque Reef
Zazil-Ha
23
CARIBBEAN SEA
Playa Norte
1
5
Centro de Convenciones
Carlos Lazo
Sección Rocas
Playa Pancholo
2
Bus Stop
Guerrero
Carlos Lazo
Post Office
10
21
Abasolo
Malecón
16
Cemetery
17
9
20
López Mateos
Plaza Isla Mujeres
22
7
Internet
Medical Center (Hyperbaric Chamber)
19
Pepe's Moto Rent
Playa Norte
15
Juárez
Guerrero
Morelos
Lighthouse
13
4
24
Matamoros
Madero
18
14
Abasolo
Juárez
Hidalgo
Plaza
Av Rueda Medina
David (Bicycle Rental)
Bravo
11
Gas Station
6
Morelos
12
3
HSBC
Bus Stop
Taxi Stand
Allende
8
Uribe
Bahía de Mujeres
Ferry to Puerto Juárez (30 min)
Ferries to Cancún's Zona Hotelera (30 min)
To Car Ferry to Punta Sam (400m); Isla Mujeres Turtle Farm (3.5km); Hacienda Mundaca (4km); Southern Beaches (5-7km); Hotel Garrafón de Castilla (5.5km); Maya Ruins (7km); Lighthouse (7km)

SUNSET GRILL *Seafood* $$$

☎ 998-877-07-85; Playa Norte at Av Rueda Media; 8am-11pm; V

This is a romantic spot for sunset cocktails and maybe even a beachside meal. While the menu runs the gamut – from seafood to pasta – the Caribbean black grouper is especially tasty. There's a smattering of vegetarian options on offer here, too, like crispy tofu with sautéed veggies.

VIVA CUBA LIBRE *Cuban* $$

Hidalgo; 5pm-midnight Tue-Sun

Take a well-deserved break from Mexican fare with *ropa vieja* (slow-cooked shredded beef), Cuban lobster and other Caribbean favorites. Mojitos are two for M$50. Viva Cuba indeed!

XPRESS SUPER *Market* $

Plaza

This chain supermarket on the plaza has all the fixings you'll need for a beachfront picnic, plus you'll save a bit of money to pay for drinks at El Patio later in the afternoon.

DRINK

Isla Mujeres' highest concentration of nightlife is along Hidalgo. Hot spots on or near the beach form an arc around the northern edge of town.

EL PATIO *Bar*

Hidalgo; 7am-11pm

This fun spot has a sand floor and an open-air back patio. There's occasional live music and the food's worth checking out.

PLAYA SOL *Bar*

Playa Norte; 9am-10pm or later

A happening spot day and night, with volleyball, a soccer area and good food and drinks at decent prices, Playa Sol is great spot to

WORTH THE TRIP: ISLA CONTOY

Spectacular Isla Contoy is a bird-lover's delight: a national park and sanctuary that is an easy day trip from Isla Mujeres. About half a mile at its widest point and more than 4 miles long, it has dense foliage that provides ideal shelter for more than 100 species of bird, including brown pelicans, olive cormorants, turkeys, brown boobies and frigate birds. Bring binoculars, mosquito repellent and sun block.

To get there, arrange a trip on Isla Mujeres with one of the scuba operations (see p60) or the **Fisherman's Cooperative** (p59). The trip gives you about two hours of free time to explore the island's two interpretive trails and to climb the 90ft-high observation tower, and you generally stop for snorkeling en route. **Amigos de Isla Contoy** (www.islacontoy.org) has a website with good information on the island's ecology.

Trip the light fantastic at La Luna DAVID PEEVERS

watch the sunset. In high season bands play reggae, salsa, merengue or other danceable music.

POC-NA HOSTEL Bar

cnr Matamoros & Carlos Lazo; sunset-sunrise

This hostel has a great beachfront joint with bonfires and more hippies than all the magic buses in the world. It's a scene, but it's a cool, chilled-out scene.

PLAY

FAYNE'S Live Music

Hidalgo; 5pm-midnight

This disco-bar-restaurant often features live reggae, salsa and other Caribbean sounds. It's a fun place and a genuine '10' on the decibel meter.

HOTEL NA BALAM Live Music

Zazil-Ha; 5pm-midnight

Caters to an older set and has a beach bar popular on weekend afternoons (every other week in the off season), with live music, dancing and a long happy hour.

LA LUNA Dance Club

Guerrero; 7am-3am or later

This club features the sound of waves, lots of wood and a nice pool table. Off the north side of the plaza, it has a great atmosphere and a fabulous mix of music. Some say it's the best in town.

>PLAYA DEL CARMEN

Playa del Carmen is the hippest city on all of the Yucatán Peninsula. Sitting coolly on the lee side of Cozumel, the town's beaches are jammed with superfit Europeans. The waters aren't as clear as those of Cancún or Cozumel – and the beach sands aren't quite as champagne powder perfect as they are further north – but still Playa (as it's locally known) continues to draw in visitors.

Strolling down Playa del Carmen's pedestrian mall, Quinta Av (5 Av), is a fabulous game of see and be seen. It's where the beautiful people go – a city of fashion and fitness, understated chic and European cool.

The town is ideally located: close to Cancún's international airport, but far enough south to allow easy access to Cozumel, Tulum, Cobá and other worthy destinations. The reefs here are excellent, too, allowing diving and snorkeling close by.

PLAYA DEL CARMEN

DO

Alltournative 1 C3
Dive Mike 2 B4
Fisherman's Cooperative 3 D3
International House 4 C3
Phocea Riviera Maya 5 C4
Playa Lingua del Caribe 6 C2
Scuba Playa 7 C4
Spa Real 8 D3
Yucatek Divers 9 A4

SHOP

Parque Turístico Leona Vicario 10 A4

EAT

Asadero Olmeca 11 A4
Babe's 12 B3
Babe's 13 D1
Buenos Aires 14 B4
Club Náutico Tarraya 15 B5
El Cuerna de Oro 16 A4
El Diez 17 D1
El Fogón 18 A3
John Gray's Place 19 C3
Restaurant 100% Natural 20 C3
Señor Tacombi 21 B3
Yaxche 22 C2

DRINK

Fusion 23 B4
La Fé 24 D2
Reina Roja 25 C2
Ula-Gula 26 B3

PLAY

Blue Parrot Bar 27 C4
Fah 28 B4
Playa 69 .... 29 B4

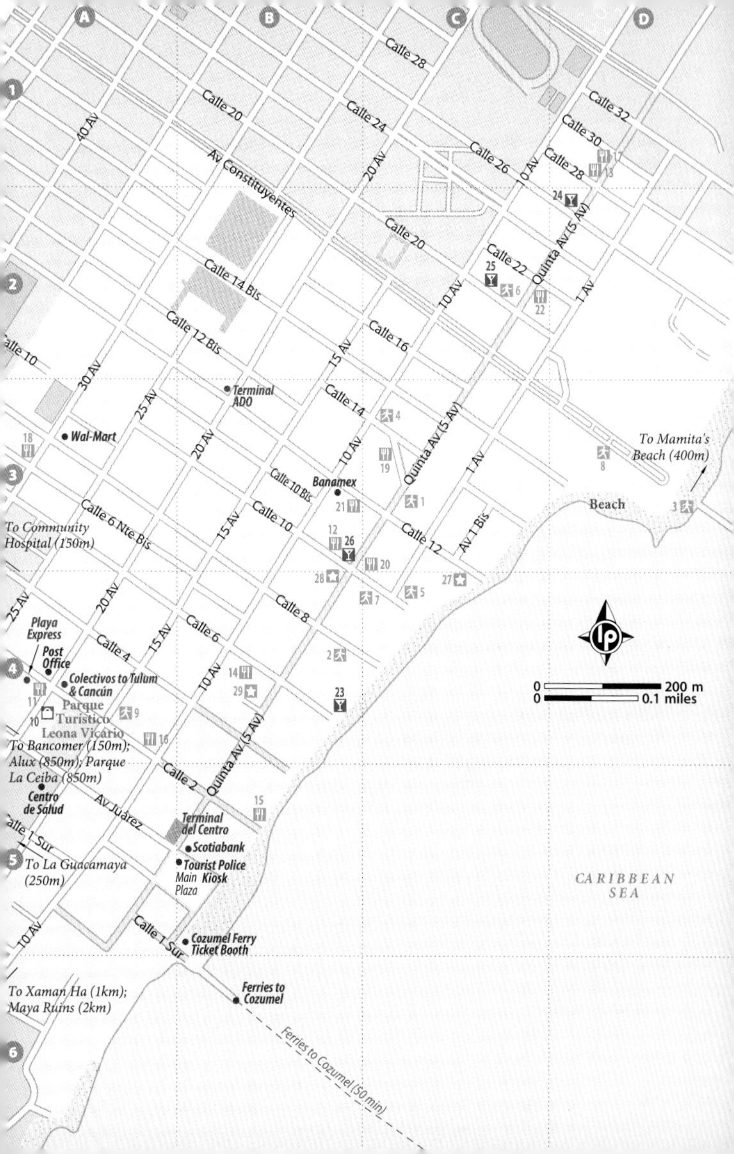

A
B
C
D
1
2
3
4
5
6
Calle 28
Calle 20
Calle 24
Calle 32
Calle 30
Calle 26
Calle 28
40 Av
20 Av
10 Av
Av Constituyentes
Quinta Av (5 Av)
Calle 20
Calle 22
Calle 14 Bis
10 Av
1 Av
Calle 12 Bis
Calle 16
Calle 10
30 Av
15 Av
Terminal ADO
25 Av
Calle 14
Wal-Mart
20 Av
10 Av
Quinta Av (5 Av)
1 Av
To Mamita's Beach (400m)
Calle 10 Bis
Banamex
Beach
Calle 6 Nte Bis
15 Av
Calle 10
Calle 12
Av 1 Bis
To Community Hospital (150m)
25 Av
20 Av
Calle 8
Playa Express
Calle 6
Calle 4
15 Av
Post Office
10 Av
Colectivos to Tulum & Cancún
Parque Turístico Leona Vicario
200 m
0.1 miles
To Bancomer (150m); Alux (850m); Parque La Ceiba (850m)
Quinta Av (5 Av)
Calle 2
Centro de Salud
Av Juárez
Terminal del Centro
Calle 1 Sur
Scotiabank
To La Guacamaya (250m)
Tourist Police Kiosk
Main Plaza
CARIBBEAN SEA
10 Av
Calle 1 Sur
Cozumel Ferry Ticket Booth
To Xaman Ha (1km); Maya Ruins (2km)
Ferries to Cozumel
Ferries to Cozumel (50 min)

SEE

Beachgoers will agree that it's pretty darn nice here. You can swim on Playa's lovely beaches nearly anywhere: just head down to the ocean, stretch out and enjoy. Many restaurants front the beach in the tourist zone; flag down a waiter if you need something frosty to beat the heat. If crowds aren't your thing, go north of Calle 28, where a few scrawny palms serve for shade.

MAMITA'S BEACH

Mamita's Beach, north of Calle 28, is considered the best place to free the girls (though going topless is generally frowned upon elsewhere in Mexico – except by the horny spring breakers, of course). There's a jazz fest here in November.

DO

Families might consider visiting a nearby ecopark (see opposite).

Most dive and snorkel outfits have similar pricing: resort dives (M$1300), one tank (M$637), two tanks (M$1027), cenote (M$1287), snorkeling (M$377), whale-shark tour to Holbox (M$3120) and open-water certification (M$4485).

ALLTOURNATIVE *Tours*

☎ 984-803-99-99; www.alltournative.com; Quinta Av; 9am-7pm Mon-Sat

Offers packages including zip-lining, rappelling and kayaking, as well as custom-designed trips. It also takes you to nearby Maya villages for an 'authentic' experience, which could easily be had on your own.

DIVE MIKE *Water Sports*

☎ 984-803-12-28; www.divemike.com; Calle 8

Offers diving and snorkeling tours by boat to a secluded reef and beach. This shop has been around forever.

GETTING THERE & AWAY

Cancún Playa Express (Calle 2 Nte) offers a quick service to downtown Cancún for M$34.

Cozumel Ferries to Cozumel (M$140 one way) leave at 6am, 8am, 9am, 10am, 11am, 1pm, 3pm, 5pm, 6pm, 7pm, 9pm and 11pm. The air-conditioned catamaran takes about a half-hour, depending on weather. Buy tickets at the booth on Calle 1 Sur. An open-air boat (same ticket price but running less regularly) takes 45 minutes to an hour; it operates mostly in the summer season.

Tulum *Colectivos* are a great option for cheap travel southward to Tulum (M$35, 45 minutes). They depart from Calle 2 near 20 Av as soon as they are full (about every 10 or 15 minutes) from 5am to 10pm. They will stop anywhere along the highway between Playa and Tulum, charging a minimum of M$15.

ECOPARK EXPLORER

There are several ecological theme parks between Playa and Tulum. They offer some of the most beautiful lagoons, cenotes and natural areas on the coast – many have also been accused of having questionable environmental records, which include allegations of dynamiting the reefs at Xcaret, as documented by www.planeta.com. Here's a quick breakdown if you decide to go.

Aktunchen (☎ 984-806-49-62; www.aktunchen.com; Carretera a Tulum Km 107; cave M$325, cenote M$260, canopy tour M$468; 9am-6pm) This inland park offers caves, cenotes and canopy tours.

Xcaret (☎ 998-883-04-70; www.xcaret.com; admission adult/child 5-12yr M$897/448.50; 8:30am-9pm;) Located 6 miles south of Playa del Carmen, Xcaret (shkar-*et*) has been turned into a heavily Disneyfied ecopark. For an additional fee you can swim with captive dolphins, take a Snuba (diving with a top-side air source that's safer for the whole family) or shark tour, or check out cultural performances. On-site there's a small, well-done artisan museum, called La Casa del Arte Popular Mexicano.

Xel-Há (☎ 998-884-71-65; www.xel-ha.com; basic admission adult/child 5-11yr M$1012/506; 9am-6pm;) A pristine lagoon brimming with iridescent tropical fish, Xel-Há (shell-hah) has landscaped grounds, developed cenotes, caves, nature paths, underwater walks with oxygen helmet (at additional cost), several restaurant-bars and more. Just 300ft south of the theme park is a small Maya ruin, also called Xel-Há (admission M$37), where you'll find a few cenotes and a rather uninspired grouping of ceremonial platforms and temples.

Xplor (☎ 998-849-52-75; www.xplor.travel; admission adult/child 5-12yr M$1336/668; 8:30am-9pm;) Located 2 miles south of Playa, Xcaret's sister resort has amphibious four-wheelers (that can't be good for the environment), underground rafts, a zip line, caves and a lagoon.

FISHERMAN'S COOPERATIVE *Water Sports*

cell phone ☎ 984-1309892; kabulyuc@hotmail.com; 4hr trip M$2000

Playa used to be a fishing village and you can still go out on small skiffs in search of kingfish, tarpon, barracuda and maybe even a sailfish. April to July is the best time.

INTERNATIONAL HOUSE *Courses*

☎ 984-803-33-88; www.ihrivieramaya.com; Calle 14; 20hr course M$2860

Offers homestays (the best way to learn a language), a small residence hall and Spanish lessons, making for a unique learning opportunity.

PHOCEA RIVIERA MAYA *Water Sports*

☎ 984-873-12-10; www.phoceariviera maya.com; 1 Av

French, English and Spanish are spoken at this central dive shop, which offers tons of options for divers of all abilities.

SWEATING OUT THOSE EVIL SPIRITS IN A MAYA TEMASCAL

The sweat lodge has always been a cornerstone of indigenous American spiritual life. The Maya, like their brothers to the north, were no different, using the temascal for both ceremonial and curative purposes.

The word 'temascal' derives from the Aztec words *teme* (to bathe) and *calli* (house). The Maya people used these bathhouses not just to keep clean, but also to heal any number of ailments. Most scholars say they were most likely used during childbirth as well. Large bath complexes have been discovered at several Maya archaeological sites. Ironically, the hygienically suspect conquistadors considered the temascales dirty places and strongholds of sin. To this day, they are used by the Maya (and tourists) to bathe and keep those evil spirits away.

PLAYA LINGUA DEL CARIBE *Courses*

☎ 984-873-38-76; www.playalingua.com; Calle 20; 20hr course M$2860

There's on-site lodging and homestays available here, too. It also offers occasional classes in Maya language, stone carving, cooking and even salsa dancing.

SCUBA PLAYA *Water Sports*

☎ 984-803-31-23; www.scubaplaya.com; Calle 10

This up-and-comer is a PADI Five Star Resort, with new equipment, professional staff and lots of shiny logos. The dives they offer aren't half bad either.

SPA REAL *Spa*

☎ 984-881-73-11; www.realresorts.com; Av Constituyentes 1

This is one of the nicer resort spas open to the public. And it offers beachside massages… Daddy like!

XAMAN HA *Bird Sanctuary*

☎ 984-873-03-30; www.aviarioxamanha.com; adult/under 12yr M$300/free; Paseo Xaman Ha Lote 1, Mz 13a, Playacar

Walk about half a mile south of town into the gated Playacar development to visit this bird sanctuary, home to some 25 distinct species. While you're in Playacar, take the time to visit the numerous unnamed **Maya ruins** found along the main drag.

YUCATEK DIVERS *Water Sports*

☎ 984-803-13-63; www.yucatek-divers.com; 15 Av

This good dive shop has German-, French-, English-, Spanish- and Dutch-speaking staff and offers limited-mobility dives for travelers with disabilities.

SHOP

PARQUE LA CEIBA *Market*

www.florafaunaycultura.org; Calle 1 Sur & Diagonal 60, Colonia Ejidal; 7am-9pm Tue-Sun

There's a cultural fair the third Saturday of each month (Sábado de Tianguis) at this great little green space, where you'll also find a recycling center (unheard of in this part of Mexico), cultural meeting rooms and a reclaimed green area that the non-profit organization Flora, Fauna y Cultura is using to bring a little nature into the lives of everyday *playenses.*

PARQUE TURÍSTICO LEONA VICARIO *Market*

cnr Avs 15 & Juárez

There are occasional artisan fairs at this friendly little plaza. While you're there, head inland on Av Juárez for plenty of shopping at half the price – there are clothes, shoes, batteries and even artisan goods on offer.

WORTH THE TRIP: NEARBY CENOTES

On the west side of the highway south of Playa del Carmen is a series of cenotes (limestone sinkholes filled with water) that you can visit and usually swim in for a price. Among these is **Cristalino Cenote** (adult M$40; 6am-5:30pm), just south of the Barceló Maya Resort. The well-tended cenote has mangrove on one side and a large open section you can dive into by climbing a ladder up to a ledge above it. The water extends about 65ft into an overhung, cavelike portion.

Two more sinkholes, **Cenote Azul** and **El Jardín del Edén**, are just south of Cristalino along the highway. But Cristalino is the best of the three.

Quirky crafts on Quinta Av GREG BENCHWICK

QUINTA AV *Pedestrian Mall*

5 Av, btwn Calles 1 Sur & 30

There's something for nearly everyone on this long pedestrian mall, from traditional textiles you'll most often find in the Chiapas region to great silver pieces from Taxco and traditional *alebrijes* (brightly colored sculptures most commonly associated with the Oaxaca region of Mexico). And yep, there's a Señor Frog's Souvenir shop here, too.

Guadalupe Quintana

Director Flora, Fauna y Cultura

Favorite spots to find peace in Quintana Roo Our spot here, Parque La Ceiba (p70), is a great alternative for families to get together. Puerto Morelos (p52) is the oldest city in an area that has grown so much in recent years. It's surrounded by mangrove forests, and the Mesoamerican reef is also very close by. Now that's a good spot to find peace. **And what about places south of Playa?** In Sian Ka'an Biosphere Reserve (p98) the *encanto* is that there's just so little development. Further south, you have Laguna Bacalar (p107), a unique and lovely place that just seems to go on forever.

EAT

Head out of the tourist zone to find cheap, quality eats. There's a ton of food stands on Av 10 between Calles 8 and 10 near the center. On Av 30, between Calles 6 and 26, you'll find an excellent selection of seafood restaurants and *taquerías* (taco stalls) favored by locals.

ALUX *Contemporary Mexican* $$$

☎ 984-803-29-36; Av Juárez; 🕓 7pm-2am

About three blocks west of Hwy 307, the Alux is an amazing must-visit. It's a restaurant-lounge situated in a cavern: stalactites, stalagmites, pools and all. Candles and dim electric lights illuminate numerous nooks and crannies converted into sofalike seating. It offers live music nightly at 10pm.

ASADERO OLMECA

Traditional Mexican $

Calle 2; 🕓 7am-6pm

Choose between tacos, kebabs and pizza at this beloved hole in the wall. It's not the fanciest of Playa's eateries, but it's well worth a visit for an afternoon snack.

BABE'S *Asian* $$

Calle 10; 🕓 noon-11:30pm Mon-Sat, 5-11:30pm Sun; V

Babe's serves some excellent Thai food, including a yummy home-style *tom kha gai* (chicken and coconut-milk soup) brimming with veggies. Most dishes can be done vegetarian. There's another Babe's along the Nueva Quinta (the new section of Quinta Av to the north of Av Constituyentes) between Calles 28 and 30.

BUENOS AIRES

Argentinean $$$

☎ 984-873-27-51; Calle 6; 🕓 noon-11:30pm

This Argentinean-owned steak house is well known for its *parrilla,* an all-you-can-eat smorgasbord. Waiters bring your meat to you on a skewer. You can also sample ribs,

YUCATÁN FAST FACTS

Timekeepers The Maya developed two separate calendars: one with 260 days, the second a 365-day cycle that corresponds to the solar year. The two cycles match up every 52 years, a period referred to as the Long Count.

White men playing Mexicans *Viva Zapata!* (1952) stars Anthony Quinn and Marlon Brando, and traces the story of the Mexican Revolution. Quinn won an Oscar for his supporting role, while Brando, though nominated, was left out in the cold.

Sacred scribes Ah Tz'ib are the Maya scribes who wrote the sacred texts of the Maya, including the *Chilam Balam.* H-menob (shamans) and Ah Tz'ib still practice their craft throughout the peninsula.

empanadas, burgers and other 'lighter' fare.

CLUB NÁUTICO TARRAYA

Seafood $$

☎ 984-873-20-40; Calle 2; mains M$50-150; 🕒 noon-9pm

One of the few restaurants in Playa del Carmen that dates from the 1960s, this casual beachfront eatery continues to offer good seafood at decent prices.

EL CUERNA DE ORO

Traditional Mexican $

cnr Calle 2 & 10 Av; 🕒 7am-10pm

Hearty, home-style set meals are served in this casual eatery. You get a giant portion of your selected dish (the three or four options change nightly) plus rice, beans and unlimited refills of the nightly drink.

Score an outside table at El Diez GREG BENCHWICK

EL DIEZ *Argentinean* $$

cnr Quinta Av & Calle 30

In a loving nod to Diego Maradona, El Diez serves up pizzas and *parrilladas* (Argentinean-style barbecues) just the way the master would have wanted them. And the outside seating on La Nueva Quinta makes for some great people watching.

EL FOGÓN *Traditional Mexican* $

cnr 30 Av & Calle 6 Nte Bis; 🕒 noon-10pm

For authentic grilled meats, tacos and *tortas* head inland to this locally recommended restaurant. The open kitchen fills the dining area with enticing aromas – plus, you're sure that the place is clean. The meal begins with a complimentary plate of succulent *nopales* (prickly pair cactus).

JOHN GRAY'S PLACE

Contemporary $$$

☎ 984-803-36-89; www.johngrayrestaurantgroup.com; Calle Corazón 5; 🕒 6-11pm Mon-Sat

Proceed to John Gray's Place for crab cakes that melt on the tongue or seasonal dishes like chicken with cilantro pesto. It's a nice place for drinks too, with Norah Jones crooning in the background as you polish off your glass of wine from the extensive list.

Juan de la Rosa
Chef at Yaxche (p76)

Favorite traditional Maya dishes *Pavo en relleno negro* (turkey slow cooked in a black mole sauce) is absolutely delicious. *Queso relleno* (stuffed cheese) is made with Edam cheese and filled with ground pork, while *pollo en escabeche* (chicken with vinaigrette) is usually cooked in a special *recado* (a spicy regional marinade or rub). **Aside from your restaurant, where should we go to get good Maya cuisine?** People can go to either Mérida (p115) or Valladolid (p111) for a more authentic look at traditional Yucatecan cuisine.

LA GUACAMAYA
Traditional Mexican $$

cnr Calle 1 Sur & 30 Av; noon-10pm Mon-Sat, to 5pm Sun

Locals love this large open-air restaurant. Veggies beware: if it doesn't have hoofs, it's unlikely to make it on the menu. Try the *tablazo,* a monstrous mixed grill with every cut of meat imaginable.

RESTAURANT 100% NATURAL
Health Food $$

984-873-22-42; cnr Quinta Av & Calle 10; 7am-11pm; V

The trademarks of this rapidly expanding chain – vegetable- and fruit-juice blends, salads, various vegetable and chicken dishes and other healthy foods – are delicious and filling.

SEÑOR TACOMBI
Taquería $

Calle 12; 7am-10pm

This converted Volkswagen bus is one of the town's cheapest and most innovative snack shacks. Go for the tacos.

YAXCHE
Yucatecan $$

984-873-25-02; www.mayacuisine.com; cnr Calle 22 & Quinta Av; noon-10pm

A good introduction to the delicious food found in the Maya countryside, Yaxche gets a bit over the top with occasional live traditional performances, but the food is pretty darned good.

DRINK

Venues here come and go, so ask around if you're wondering where the party is (or where it isn't). You'll find everything from mellow, tranced-out lounge bars to classic rock-and-roll places. The party generally starts on Quinta Av, then heads down toward the beach on Calle 10. There's an art walk, where local artists come to display their work, almost every night on Quinta Av.

FUSION
Lounge

Calle 6; until late

Groove out beachside under that Playa moon at Fusion, one of our favorite beachfront lounges in all the Riviera Maya. There's live music most nights and the beachside eating is worth checking out.

LA FÉ
Bar

cnr Quinta Av & Calle 26; 11am-4am;

This Nueva Quinta bar caters to a younger hipster crowd. If you don't want to jam out to the likes of the Pixies and The Clash, then you might want to consider another spot.

REINA ROJA
Lounge

Calle 20; until late

Turn on the red light at this odd-ball lounge that has its own swimming pool, private karaoke

WORTH THE TRIP: EXPLORING THE RIVIERA MAYA

There's plenty to do south of Playa along the Riviera Maya. Here are some top tips.

Akumal Just 23 miles south of Playa, this excellent resort area offers up great snorkeling at the Laguna Yal-Kú, plus educational opportunities at the Ecological Center (www.ceakumal.org).

Cenote Dos Ojos (www.aquacaves.com) Just half a mile south of Xel-Há (p69), this cenote offers great snorkeling. From here, divers can explore the third-largest underwater cave system in the world.

Hidden Worlds (www.hiddenworlds.com.mx) Just south of Dos Ojos, this cenote has diving and snorkeling, plus a 'junglemobile' that'll take you there.

Paamul (www.paamul.com.mx) About 15 miles south of Playa, this beach attracts turtles in July and August, and vacationing snowbirds in the winter.

Rancho Punta Venado (www.puntavenado.com) Three miles south of Xcaret (p69), you'll find this low-key operation that focuses on horseback riding.

Tankah (www.tankah.com) This laid-back beach town is just north of Tulum. It features a series of seven interconnecting cenotes.

Xcacel-Xcacelito Located at Km 112 of the Cancún-Tulum Hwy, this beach has a sea-turtle operation, a cenote and good snorkeling at its north end.

rooms and occasional movies. American rock dominates despite the fashionista vibe.

ULA-GULA *Lounge*

cnr Quinta Av & Calle 10; 11am-2am

Creative cocktails – try the *paloma* (tequila, grapefruit juice and fizz), one of the best in town – make this mod corner bar a must on your nightly pub crawl.

PLAY

BLUE PARROT BAR *Dance Club*

984-873-00-83; Calle 12; 11am-4am

This is the Blue Parrot Inn's immensely popular open-sided *palapa* beachfront bar with swing chairs, a giant outdoor dance stage, indoor section if the weather's bad and lots of sand.

FAH *Live Music*

Quinta Av; until 2am

A friendly open-air bar with some of the best live music in town, Fah gets going early, making it a good spot for early drinks (after all, it's afternoon somewhere in the world).

PLAYA 69 *GLBT Entertainment*

Callejón, off Quinta Av; www.rivieramayagay.com; until late Tue-Sun

This gay disco has erratic hours and normally gets going late. The *jueves de carne* (Beefcake Thursdays) strip show is sure to get your heart pumping.

>COZUMEL

A hugely popular diving spot since 1961, when Jacques Cousteau, led by local guides, showed its spectacular reefs to the world, Cozumel is Quintana Roo's largest island. Called Ah-Cuzamil-Peten (Island of Swallows) by its earliest inhabitants, Cozumel has become a world-famous diving and cruise-ship destination.

While diving and snorkeling are the main draws, San Miguel de Cozumel, the main tourist zone on the island, offers lots of shopping 'deals' (often not very cheap) and a pleasant town square in which to spend the afternoon. In February there is a festive Carnaval, which brings dancers festooned with feathers out into the streets. And you'll definitely want to rent a scooter or VW bug for the day to cruise the less-visited, windswept far side of the island, which has beautiful beaches and a few large waves. Along the way, you can get wet at pristine coastal parks, tour a few Maya ruins and groove out at roadside Rasta bars.

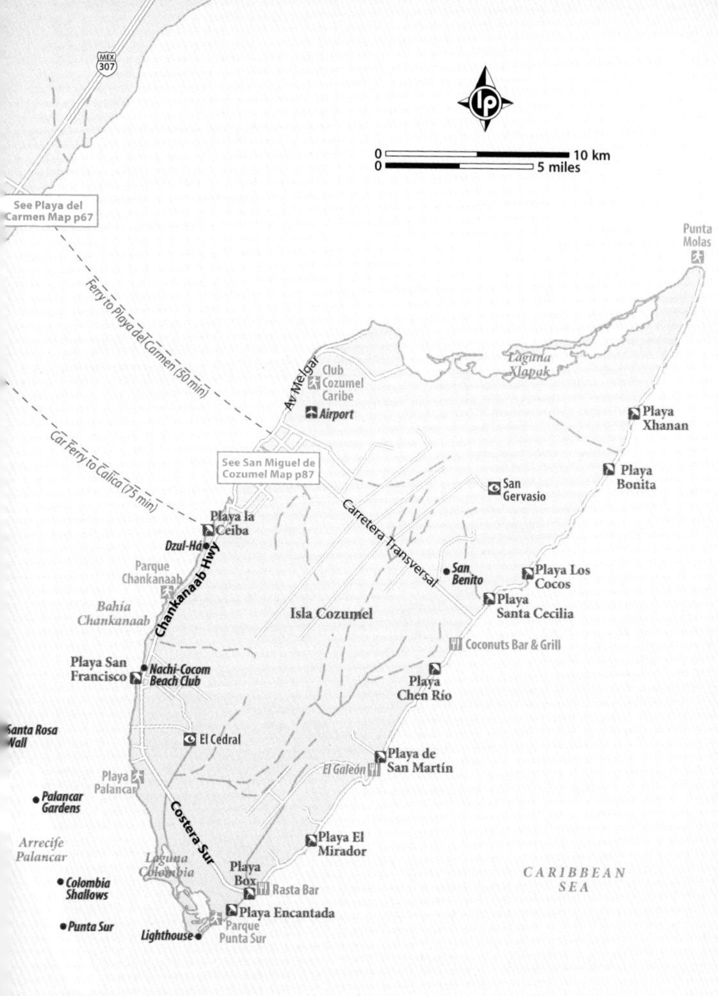

MEX 307
0
10 km
0
5 miles
See Playa del Carmen Map p67
Punta Molas
Ferry to Playa del Carmen (50 min)
Car Ferry to Calica (75 min)
Av Melgar
Club Cozumel Caribe
Airport
Laguna Xlapak
Playa Xhanan
Playa Bonita
See San Miguel de Cozumel Map p87
San Gervasio
Carretera Transversal
Playa la Ceiba
Dzul-Há
Chankanaab Hwy
Parque Chankanaab
Bahía Chankanaab
San Benito
Playa Los Cocos
Playa Santa Cecilia
Isla Cozumel
Coconuts Bar & Grill
Playa San Francisco
Nachi-Cocom Beach Club
Playa Chen Río
Santa Rosa Wall
El Cedral
Playa de San Martín
El Galeón
Playa Palancar
Palancar Gardens
Costera Sur
Arrecife Palancar
Playa El Mirador
Laguna Colombia
Playa Box
Rasta Bar
CARIBBEAN SEA
Colombia Shallows
Playa Encantada
Parque Punta Sur
Punta Sur
Lighthouse

SEE

MUSEO DE LA ISLA DE COZUMEL

987-872-14-34; Av Melgar; admission M$36; 8am-5pm

Exhibits at this fine museum in San Miguel present a clear and detailed picture of the island's flora, fauna, geography, geology and ancient Maya history.

DO

Cozumel has some of the best snorkeling and diving in the world. It has fantastic year-round visibility (commonly 100ft or more) and a jaw-droppingly impressive variety of marine life that includes spotted eagle rays, moray eels, groupers, barracudas, turtles, sharks, brain coral and huge sponges. The island has strong currents (normally around 3 knots), making drift dives the standard, especially along the many walls. Prices vary, but in general expect to pay about M$950 for a two-tank dive (less if you bring your own buoyancy control device and regulator), M$910 for an introductory 'resort' course and M$5460 for PADI open-water certification. For more tips on diving, see p124.

CLUB COZUMEL CARIBE *Beach Club*

800-833-59-71; www.clubcozumelcaribe.info

This beach club has underwater cement statuary that makes for some interesting snorkeling. It has a decent beach and pool and, as of press time, you don't need to pay anything to get in. It also has a climbing wall.

DEEP BLUE *Water Sports*

987-872-56-53; www.deepbluecozumel.com; cnr Av 10 Sur & Dr Rosado Salas

This PADI operation has very good gear and fast boats that give you a chance to get more dives out of a day. It also offers snorkeling tours. A half-day snorkeling tour will cost from M$400 to M$650. The Arrecife Palancar (Palancar Reef) or the adjacent Colombia Shallows, near the island's southern end, are some of the best offshore spots.

EAGLE RIDER *Motorcycle Rental*

Av Juárez

Cruise the island in style with the scooters (M$455), dirt bikes and motorcycles (M$845 to M$975), Harleys (from M$1560) and dune buggies (M$715) from this downtown shop.

RENTADORA ISIS *Scooter & Car Rental*

987-872-33-67; Av 5 Nte

A well-respected rental shop that lends out old convertible VW Beetles for around M$400. Scooters

Deborah Felixson

Owner-Manager, Deep Blue (opposite)

Favorite diving spot for all levels Any section on Palancar (p88) is great. There are giant coral formations. Colombia Shallows gives you the sensation of being in an aquarium. It's just 30ft below the surface, with great clarity of water, and the colors are amazingly vibrant. **What about diving spots for pros?** La Garganta del Diablo (The Devil's Throat) at Punta Sur is one of the most dramatic dives around. You enter through a tunnel forged from red coral at 100ft, dropping down at a 45-degree angle to the exit at 125ft. In all of Quintana Roo, Cozumel is probably the best spot for diving. You just can't compare. There's nothing like the walls and 65ft-long columns we have here.

TRACING THE ISLAND'S HISTORY

Maya settlement on Cozumel dates from AD 300. During the post-Classic period, Cozumel flourished as a trade center and, more importantly, a ceremonial site. Every Maya woman living on the Yucatán Peninsula and beyond was expected to make at least one pilgrimage to Cozumel to pay tribute to Ixchel, the goddess of fertility and the moon, at a temple erected in her honor. Archaeologists believe this temple was at San Gervasio, a bit northeast of the island's geographical center.

At the time of the first Spanish contact with Cozumel (in 1518, by Juan de Grijalva and his men), there were at least 32 Maya building groups on the island. According to Spanish chronicler Diego de Landa, a year later Hernán Cortés sacked one of the Maya centers but left the others intact, apparently satisfied with converting the island's population to Christianity. Smallpox introduced by the Spanish wiped out half the 8000 Maya and, of the survivors, only about 200 escaped genocidal attacks by conquistadors in the late 1540s.

The island remained virtually deserted into the late 17th century, its coves providing sanctuary for several notorious pirates, including Jean Lafitte and Henry Morgan. In 1848 indigenous people fleeing the War of the Castes began to resettle Cozumel. At the beginning of the 20th century, the island's (by then mostly *mestizo*) population grew, thanks to the craze for chewing gum. Cozumel was a port of call on the chicle export route and locals harvested the gum base on the island. After the demise of chicle, Cozumel's economy remained strong due to the construction of a US air base during WWII.

When the US military departed, the island fell into an economic slump and many of its people moved away. Those who stayed fished for a living until 1961, when Cousteau's documentary broadcast Cozumel's glorious sea life to the world. The tourists began arriving almost overnight.

start at M$220. Keep in mind that the winds are strong on the other side of the island. If you are not used to riding a scooter, you may wish to stick with the little love bug.

SCUBA CLUB COZUMEL *Water Sports*

☎ 987-872-08-53; www.scubaclubcozumel.com; Av Melgar Sur 1251

This PADI Five Star Dive Center has been in business for around 30 years. It has seven boats and good knowledge of local dive spots.

SNORKELING *Water Sports*

Good snorkeling can be found at Casitas just north of San Miguel de Cozumel, and Dzul-Há, Parque Chankanaab, Playa Palancar and Parque Punta Sur to the south.

TOURIST INFORMATION OFFICE *Tours*

2nd fl, La Plaza del Sol; 8am-3pm Mon-Fri

You may be able to get some information at the main tourist office, located in the La Plaza del Sol; otherwise, head to its kiosks at the cruise-ship dock or at the Plaza Langosta mall (below), just opposite the cruise-ship dock.

 SHOP

There's plenty of shopping around San Miguel's main plaza and along Av Melgar.

FAMA *Books*

☎ 987-872-50-20; Av 5 Nte; 9am-10pm

This chain carries books and periodicals in English and Spanish. It's not the type of selection that will knock your intellectual socks off, rather it's a good spot for beach books and other mindless entertainment.

PLAZA LANGOSTA *Mall*

Av Melgar

There's a good grouping of shops in this American-style mall. It's as brightly lit and shiny as anything you'll find in the States or Europe, with prices to match.

 EAT

COCINA ECONÓMICA LAS PALMAS *Traditional Mexican* $

cnr Calle 3 Sur & Av 25 Sur; 9:30am-7pm Mon-Sat

This place packs with locals come lunchtime. And although it gets hotter than Hades, you'll love the *chicharrones* (fried pork rinds) and Maya favorites like *poc chuc* (slow-roasted pork) on offer.

COCINA MEXICANA LOS RÍOS *Traditional Mexican* $

cnr Av 5 Sur & Calle 7 Sur; 7am-5pm Mon-Sat

Ceviches, chicken and seafood: all simple and good. Red plastic furniture and Bellafonte tunes are part of this cheap, clean cafe not far from the post office. *Comida corridas* are M$35 (a smokin' deal) and get you a main, a soup, tortillas, a soda or other nonalcoholic drink and dessert.

COFFEELIA *Cafe* $

☎ 987-872-74-02; Calle 5 Sur; 7:30am-11pm Mon-Sat, 8am-1pm Sun; V

A great way to start or finish the day is to head over to Coffeelia for warm smiles, delicious food and great coffees. The menu includes quiche, good salads and vegetarian dishes. Thursday is story night in the pleasant garden area.

COSTA BRAVA *Seafood* $$

☎ 987-869-00-93; Calle 7 Sur 57; 6:30am-11pm

Painted in bright, preschool primary colors, this casual place with its

WORTH THE TRIP: EXPLORING THE REST OF THE ISLAND

In order to see most of the island you will have to rent a vehicle or take a taxi (M$700 to M$1000 for a day trip); cyclists will need to brave the regular strong winds. The following route will take you south from San Miguel, then counterclockwise around the island; see the Cozumel map, Map p79.

Parque Chankanaab (admission M$208; 7am-6pm;) A popular snorkeling spot. However, there's not a lot to see in the water beyond some brightly colored fish and deliberately sunken artificial objects. The beach is a nice one, though, and 150ft inland is a limestone lagoon surrounded by iguanas and inhabited by turtles. There's a small archaeological park containing replica Olmec heads and Maya artifacts, a small museum featuring objects from Chichén Itzá, and a botanical garden with 400 species of tropical plants.

El Cedral (admission free) This Maya ruin is the oldest on the island. It's the size of a small house and has no ornamentation. It's 2 miles down a signed paved road that heads off to the left (east) a half-mile or two south of Nachi-Cocom Beach Club's access road.

Playa Palancar About 10 miles south of town, this is another great spot with a beach club renting hydro bikes, kayaks, snorkel gear and sailboats, plus a restaurant and a dive operation.

Parque Punta Sur (987-872-09-14; admission M$130; 9am-5pm) Visitors to this ecopark on the southern tip of the island board an open vehicle for the 2-mile ride to visit picturesque Celarain lighthouse and the small nautical museum at its base. Another vehicle carries visitors to Laguna Colombia, part of a three-lagoon system that is the habitat of crocodiles and many resident and migratory waterfowl.

East Coast The eastern shoreline is the wildest part of the island and presents some beautiful seascapes and many small blowholes (there's a bunch around Km 30.5). Swimming is dangerous on most of the east coast because of riptides and undertows. With a bit of care you can sometimes swim at Punta Chiqueros, Playa Chen Río and Punta Morena. As you travel along the coast, consider stopping for lunch or a drink at the Rasta Bar (Km 29.5), El Galeón (Km 43.1) or Coconuts Bar & Grill (Km 43.5). El Galeón rents surf and body boards for M$260 and M$80 per hour, respectively. Or just bring a picnic lunch and plan on having the beach to yourself.

Punta Molas Adventurous types may want to consider taking a rental ATV (all-terrain vehicle) – or hoofing it – up the road to Punta Molas on the island's northeast shore. The road is closed to regular cars, but locals report that you can get there by ATV. Try it out, but be sure to bring plenty of water.

San Gervasio (admission M$90; 7am-4pm) This Maya complex is Cozumel's only preserved ruins. It is thought to have been the site of the sanctuary of Ixchel, goddess of the moon and fertility, and thus an important pilgrimage site at which Maya women – in particular prospective mothers – worshipped. But its structures are small and crude, and the clay idols of Ixchel were long ago destroyed by the Spaniards.

lovely Virgencita shrine has good prices on lobster dishes, chicken and shrimp.

JEANNIE'S *Waffle House* $$

☎ 987-878-46-47; cnr Av Melgar & Calle 11 Sur; 7am-7pm

The views of the water are great from the outdoor patio. Jeannie's serves waffles, plus hash-brown potatoes, eggs, sandwiches and other tidbits like vegetarian fajitas. Great frozen coffees beat the midday heat.

LA COCAY *Contemporary* $$$

987-872-55-33; Calle 8 Nte 208; 5-11pm Mon-Sat

Romantic, coconut-scented candlelight and an intimate atmosphere make this snazzy restaurant a lot of fun. Sit at the bar sipping a good single malt or find a quiet table in the corner (or the back garden) to chat with someone special. The menu changes seasonally, but focuses on light, Mediterranean-influenced fare.

LOS DORADOS DE VILLA *Traditional Mexican* $$

☎ 987-872-01-96; Calle 1 Sur; 8am-midnight

Near the edge of the main plaza, this airy spot specializes in food from the Distrito Federal (Mexico City and surroundings), but has a wide variety of Mexican dishes, including seafood and cuts of meat.

YUCATÁN FAST FACTS

Celestial body Ixchel, the moon and fertility goddess, was the principal female deity of the Maya pantheon. Today she is linked with the Virgin Mary.

Deep Down The *Cozumel Dive Guide* (www.cozumeldiveguide.com) offers great maps and descriptions of the area's dives. Lonely Planet has a dive guide to the region, too: *Cozumel: Diving & Snorkeling*.

Thank you Mel...we think Mel Gibson's Oscar-nominated *Apocalypto* hit theaters in 2006 and was the first ever major film in the Yucatec Maya language. It was filmed mostly in Veracruz.

The spinach crêpes are great, as are the complimentary chips.

MEGA *Market* $

cnr Av Melgar & Calle 11 Sur

Head to this large supermarket to pimp out your picnic lunch. They don't call it Mega for nothing: you can find everything under the sun, even snorkels and goggles if you forgot yours on the boat.

MERCADO MUNICIPAL *Market* $

Dr Rosado Salas

Cheapest of all eating places are the little market *loncherías* (lunch stalls) next to the Mercado Municipal. Most offer soup and a main course for around M$35 to M$40, with a large selection of dishes available; ask about the cheap *comida corrida* (fixed-price menu) not listed on the menu.

PANCHO'S BACKYARD
Seafood $$$

987-872-21-41; cnr Av Melgar & Calle 8 Nte; 10am-11pm Mon-Sat, 4-10:30pm Sun

Very atmospheric and set in a beautifully decorated inner courtyard, Pancho's has decent food that focuses on international favorites and (drumroll please) seafood.

PASTELERÍA Y PANADERÍA ZERMATT
Bakery $

cnr Av 5 Nte & Calle 4 Nte; 7am-8:30pm Mon-Sat

Bakes pastries, cakes, pizzas and whole-wheat breads and serves decent coffee. We only wish it had more dishes on offer, but, as they say, pick one thing and do it right.

RESTAURANT LA CHOZA
Traditional Mexican $$

987-872-09-58; cnr Dr Rosado Salas & Av 10 Sur; 7am-10:30pm

An excellent and popular restaurant specializing in authentic regional cuisine, La Choza sometimes has a budget-busting fixed meal at lunchtime.

TAQUERÍA EL SITIO
Taquería $

Calle 2 Nte; 7am-1pm

For scrumdiddlyumptious tacos and *tortas*, head over to El Sitio. It has fancied up the canopy-covered eating area with a mural of a cruise ship and jumping dolphins.

SAN MIGUEL DE COZUMEL

SEE
Museo de la Isla de Cozumel 1 C2

DO
Deep Blue 2 C4
Eagle Rider 3 C3
Rentadora Isis 4 C3
Tourist Information Office 5 C3

SHOP
Fama 6 C3
Plaza Langosta 7 A4

EAT
Cocina Económica Las Palmas 8 C5
Cocina Mexicana Los Ríos 9 B4
Coffeelia 10 B4
Costa Brava 11 B4
Jeannie's 12 A4
La Cocay 13 D2
Los Dorados de Villa 14 C3
Mega 15 A4
Mercado Municipal 16 C4
Pancho's Backyard 17 D2
Pastelería y Panadería Zermatt 18 C3
Restaurant La Choza 19 C4
Taquería El Sitio 20 C3

DRINK
La Abuelita 21 C3
Woody's Bar & Grill 22 C3

PLAY
Aqua 23 D2
Estadio Javier Rojo Gomez 24 D5

A
B
C
D
1
2
3
4
5
6
400 m
0.2 miles
Ferry to Playa del Carmen (50 min)
CARIBBEAN SEA
Passenger Ferry Dock (Muelle Fiscal)
Cruise Ship Dock
Av Melgar Sur
Post Office
Clínica Médica Hiperbárica
To Scuba Club Cozumel (500m)
Tourist Police
Park
Main Plaza
Plaza del Sol
Av Benito Juárez
HSBC
Banorte
Cruz Roja
Gas Station
Calle 12 Nte
Calle 10 Nte
Calle 8 Nte
Calle 6 Nte
Calle 4 Nte
Calle 2 Nte
Calle 1 Sur
Calle 3 Sur
Calle 5 Sur
Calle 7 Sur
Calle 9 Sur
Calle 11 Sur
Calle 13 Sur
Calle 15 Sur
Calle 17 Sur
Av 5 Nte
Av 10 Nte
Av 15 Nte
Av 20 Nte
Av Juárez
Av 5 Sur
Av 5 Sur (Quinta Av)
Av 10 Sur
Av 15 Sur
Av 20 Sur
Av 25 Sur
Av 30 Sur
Av 35 Sur
Av 40 Sur
Av 55 Sur
Dr Rosado Salas
Morelos
Hidalgo
Mujica
Angeles

COZUMEL'S TOP DIVE SITES

Ask any dive operator in Cozumel to name the best dive sites in the area and the following names will come up time and again.

Santa Rosa Wall

This is the biggest of the famous sites. The wall is so large most people are able to see only a third of it on one tank. Regardless of where you're dropped, expect to find enormous overhangs and tunnels covered with coral and sponges. Stoplight parrot fish, black grouper and barracuda all hang out at this wall. The average visibility is 100ft and minimum depth 30ft, with average depths closer to 85ft. Carry a flashlight with you, even if you're diving at noon, as it will help to bring out the color of coral at depth and illuminate the critters hiding in crevices. Hurricane Wilma left shallower spots with uncovered coral, but for the most part it is unharmed.

Punta Sur

Unforgettable for its coral caverns, each of which is named, this reef is for experienced, properly certified divers only. Before you dive, be sure to ask your dive master to point out the Devil's Throat. This cave opens into a cathedral room with four tunnels, all of which make for some pretty hairy exploration. Only advanced divers should consider entering the Devil's Throat, but anyone who visits Punta Sur will be impressed by the cave system and the butterfly fish, angelfish and whip corals that abound here.

Colombia Shallows

Also known as Colombia Gardens, Colombia Shallows lends itself equally well to snorkeling and scuba diving. Because it's a shallow dive (maximum depth 30ft, average 5ft to 10ft), its massive coral buttresses covered with sponges and other resplendent life-forms are well illuminated. The current at Colombia Gardens is generally light to moderate. This and the shallow water allow you to spend hours at the site if you want and you'll never get bored spying all the elkhorn coral, pillar coral and anemones that live there.

Palancar Gardens

Also known as Palancar Shallows and thus one of the spots that sustained serious Wilma damage, this dive can be appreciated by snorkelers due to the slight current usually present and its modest maximum depth (65ft). The Gardens consists of a strip reef about 80ft wide and very long, riddled with fissures and tunnels. The major features are enormous stovepipe sponges and vivid yellow tube sponges, and you can always find damselfish, parrot fish and angelfish around you. In the deeper parts of the reef, divers will want to keep an eye out for the lovely black corals.

DRINK

LA ABUELITA *Bar*

cnr Calle 1 Sur & Av 10 Sur

Grab a drink with locals at the 'little grandma.' Turns out granny is quite an enterprising lady: there's an Abuelita Dos *and* Tres in other parts of town.

WOODY'S BAR & GRILL *Bar*

Av Juárez; until 3am

This easygoing shotgun bar near the plaza is about as friendly as you can get. While the crowd tends toward the cruise-boat Jimmy Buffet set, there's always plenty of friendly banter and the whizzing fans are a welcome cooldown after a long day of sightseeing.

PLAY

San Miguel de Cozumel's nightlife is quiet and subdued. Most restaurants are open for drinks, but by 11pm things wind down. Try the plaza or around the cruise-ship dock first.

AQUA *Live Music*

Calle 6 Nte 81

The Hotel Flamingo's lobby bar is a fairly hip spot catering to an older crowd. There's live jazz in the high season.

ESTADIO JAVIER ROJO GOMEZ *Performances*

cnr Dr Rosado Salas & Av 30 Sur

The city's stadium hosts rock concerts, *lucha libre* (professional wrestling) matches and just about any other event you can think of. Most events happen on the weekends, but ask around.

GETTING THERE & AROUND

Ferries from Playa del Carmen

Passenger ferries run to Cozumel from the pier in Playa del Carmen and arrive right in front of the main plaza. México Waterjets (www.mexicowaterjets.com) and Ultramar (www.granpuerto.com.mx) charge M$140 one way. There's normally a passenger ferry every hour to and from Cozumel, depending on the season, from 6am to midnight.

Taxis Some locals refer to the 'taxi mafia.' As in some other towns on the Yucatán Peninsula, the taxi syndicate on Cozumel wields a good bit of power. Fares in and around town are M$34 per ride; to the Zona Hotelera north or south along Av Melgar, M$80; day trip around the island, M$700 to M$1000. Luggage may cost extra. Carry exact change as drivers often 'can't' provide it.

>TULUM & AROUND

Tulum's spectacular coastline – with all its confectioner-sugar sands, jade-green water, balmy breezes and bright sun – makes it one of the top beaches in Mexico. Where else can you get all that *and* a dramatically situated Maya ruin? There's also excellent diving, fun cenotes, great snorkeling and a variety of lodgings and restaurants to fit every budget.

There is one big drawback: the town center, where the really cheap eats and best bars are found, sits right on the highway, making it feel more like a truck stop than a tropical paradise. This said, both Cobá to the west and the massive Sian Ka'an Biosphere Reserve to the south make doable day trips. And the Zona Hotelera with its laid-back restaurants and hotels (not to mention tremendous beaches) is just a few kilometers inland from the main road.

Plans to extend the runway and bring in international flights could change the face of this area forever. But for now, it's still far enough off the beaten path to retain its laid-back appeal.

TULUM & AROUND

SEE

Tulum Archaeological Site 1 D2

DO

Cenote Dive Center 2 A4
Community Tours Sian Ka'an 3 C4
El Jardín del Sol 4 C3
Zazil-Kin 5 D3

SHOP

Mexican Art Gallery 6 C2

EAT

Charlie's 7 A4
El Mariachi 8 B4
La Nave 9 B4
Salsalito Taco Shop 10 B4

DRINK

Caribe Swing 11 B4

PLAY

Divino Paraíso 12 B4

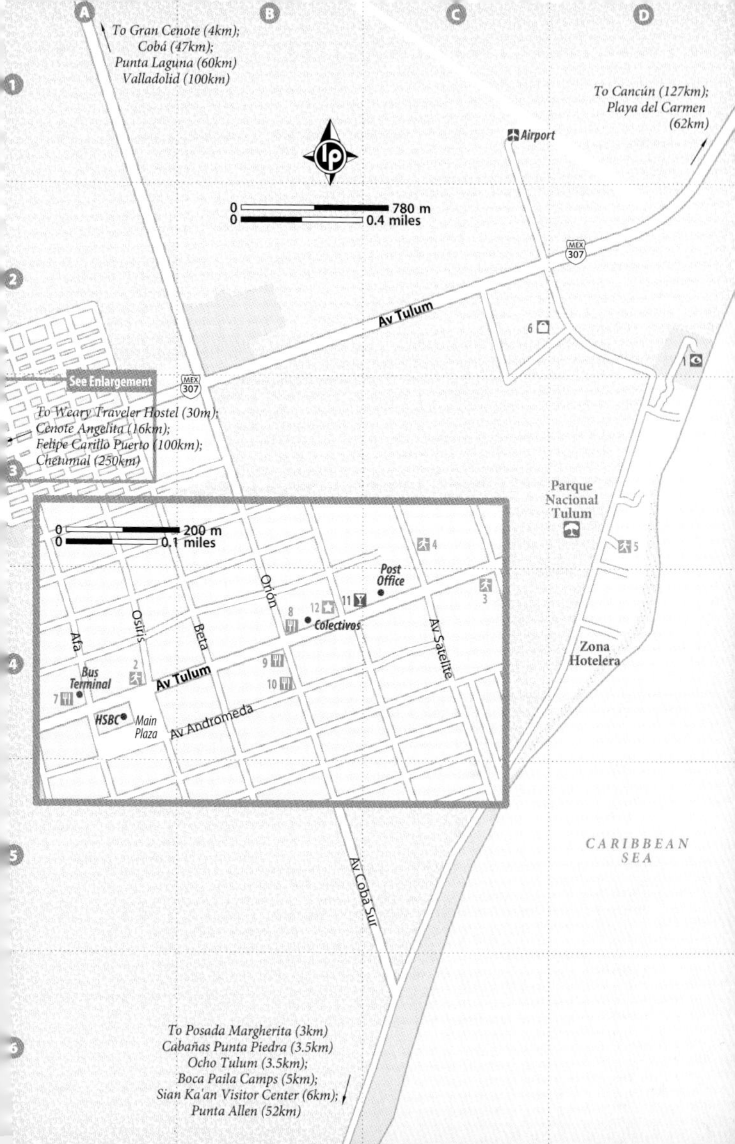

A
B
C
D
1
2
3
4
5
6
To Gran Cenote (4km); Cobá (47km); Punta Laguna (60km) Valladolid (100km)
To Cancún (127km); Playa del Carmen (62km)
Airport
0 780 m
0 0.4 miles
MEX 307
Av Tulum
6
1
See Enlargement
To Weary Traveler Hostel (30m); Cenote Angelita (16km); Felipe Carillo Puerto (100km); Chetumal (250km)
Parque Nacional Tulum
0 200 m
0 0.1 miles
4
5
3
Post Office
Orión
11
12
8
Colectivos
Av Satelite
Osiris
Beta
Afa
Zona Hotelera
9
10
2
Bus Terminal
Av Tulum
7
HSBC
Main Plaza
Av Andromeda
CARIBBEAN SEA
Av Cobá Sur
To Posada Margherita (3km) Cabañas Punta Piedra (3.5km) Ocho Tulum (3.5km); Boca Paila Camps (5km); Sian Ka'an Visitor Center (6km); Punta Allen (52km)

SEE

TULUM ARCHAEOLOGICAL SITE

admission M$51, parking M$40; 8am-4:30pm

These regal Maya ruins preside over the rugged coastline. Most archaeologists believe that Tulum was occupied during the late Postclassic period (AD 1200–1521) and that it was an important port town during its heyday. See the boxed text, opposite, for more on these ruins.

DO

There are plenty of cenotes and fun lost beaches north of Tulum on your way to Playa del Carmen. See p77 for a rundown of the best sights along the way. Ecopark goers will want to check out the parks (p69) north of here.

CABAÑAS PUNTA PIEDRA

Bike Rental

Bicycles can be a good way to get around Tulum and many hotels have them free for guests. The Punta Piedra hotel in the Zona Hotelera, south of the T-junction, rents bikes (M$80 per day) and scooters (M$400 per day).

CENOTE DIVE CENTER

Water Sports

☎ 984-876-32-85; www.cenotedive.com; Av Tulum

This recommended outfit specializes in guided cavern dives, also offering cave dives, and cenote and cavern snorkeling trips. One of the most spectacular cenote dives in the region is at **Cenote Angelita**, most notable for the unique, curious, even eerie layer of hydrogen sulfide that 'fogs' the water about halfway through the descent.

GETTING THERE & AROUND

Getting to Playa del Carmen, Punta Allen, Felipe Carrillo Puerto and Cancún
Colectivos leave from Av Tulum for Punta Allen (at 2pm) and Playa del Carmen (M$35, 45 minutes). *Colectivos* for Felipe Carrillo Puerto (M$50, one hour) leave from just south of the Weary Traveler Hostel. To get to Cancún (M$82, two hours), you're best off grabbing an ADO bus (see p148).

Getting to the beach Except for the shuttles operated from the youth hostels, there are no *colectivos* out to the beach. You either hitch, rent a taxi, ride a bike or walk. And it's a long walk (at least 30 minutes).

Taxi Cab fares are fixed and pretty cheap; it's M$40 to the ruins from either of the two taxi stands in the town center (one south of the bus terminal, which has fares posted; the other four blocks north on the opposite side of the street). The fare to the Zona Hotelera is about M$50 to M$70.

EXPLORING THE RUINS AT TULUM

Visitors are required to follow a prescribed route around the ruins. From the ticket booth, head along nearly half the length of Tulum's enormous **wall**. The **tower** at the corner, once thought to be a guard post, is now believed by some to have been a type of shrine.

Heading east you'll reach the **Casa del Cenote**, named for the small pool at its southern base, where you can sometimes see the glitter of little silvery fish as they turn sideways in the murky water. A small tomb was discovered in the cave. Walking south, you'll come across the bluff holding the **Templo del Dios del Viento** (Temple of the Wind God).

Below the Wind God's hangout is a lovely little stretch of **beach**. It's quite swimmable when conditions are good. After your dip, head west to **Estructura 25**, which has some interesting columns on its raised platform and, above the main doorway (on the south side), a beautiful stucco frieze of the Descending God. It may be related to the Maya's reverence for bees (and honey), perhaps a stylized representation of a bee sipping nectar from a flower.

South of Estructura 25 is **El Palacio**, notable for its X-figure ornamentation. From here, head east back toward the water and skirt the outside edge of the central temple complex (keeping it to your right). Heading inland again on the south side, you can enter the complex through a corbeled archway past the restored **Templo de la Estela** (Temple of the Stela), also known as the Temple of the Initial Series.

At the heart of the complex, you can admire Tulum's tallest building, a watchtower appropriately named **El Castillo** (The Castle) by the Spaniards. Note the Descending God in the middle of its facade and the Toltec-style Kukulcanes (plumed serpents) at the corners, echoing those at Chichén Itzá. To El Castillo's north is the small, lopsided **Templo del Dios Descendente**, named for the relief figure above the door.

Walking west toward the exit will take you to the two-story **Templo de las Pinturas**, constructed in several stages around AD 1400–50. Its decoration was among the most elaborate at Tulum and included relief masks and colored murals on an inner wall. The murals have been partially restored but are nearly impossible to make out. This monument might have been the last built by the Maya before the Spanish conquest and, with its columns, carvings and two-story construction, it's probably the most interesting structure at the site.

COMMUNITY TOURS SIAN KA'AN *Tours*

☎ 984-871-22-02; www.siankaantours.org; Av Tulum

Runs tours to the Sian Ka'an Biosphere Reserve (p98) that include pickup in the Zona Hotelera. Trips cost between M$910 and M$1300. There are discounts for children under 12.

EL JARDÍN DEL SOL *Yoga*

Av Satelite; eljardindelser@gmail.com

This earthy operation in the town center offers yoga courses. It's not yoga on the beach at dawn, but for those staying in the center of town this is a good bet to get your Zen on.

WORTH THE TRIP: PUNTA LAGUNA

Punta Laguna is a fair-sized lake with a small Maya community nearby, 12 miles northeast of Cobá on the road to Nuevo Xcan. The forest around the lake supports populations of spider and howler monkeys, as well as a variety of birds, and contains small, unexcavated ruins and a cenote. Surprisingly, a jaguar population was recently discovered, though chances of seeing one are very slim. Toucans sometimes flit across the road.

A **tourist cooperative** (☎ 986-107-91-87; www.puntalaguna.org) charges M$50 for entrance to the lake area, and about M$250 per hour for a guided visit, which is your best chance of spotting simians. Arrive at dusk or dawn to further increase your chances. The local community is increasing its tourist offerings in an effort to keep the town's youth from fleeing to work in Señor Froglandia. The new activities include a zip-line tour, a rappel into a nearly pitch-black cenote and a shamanic ceremony at a 'traditional' altar that's been erected fortuitously right on the trail to the lake for M$300. While these are fun, the best activity is renting a canoe (M$70 per hour) to explore the lake, an eerily beautiful sight when shrouded in morning mist.

Like any rural community, Punta Laguna offers a unique opportunity to learn about the local indigenous culture; travelers might consider studying Maya with local women (prices vary). There's a restaurant near the cenote, but it rarely opens, so consider bringing your own food.

Other options include stopping for a hike on the new nature trail in the town of **Campamento Hidalgo** (3 miles south of Punta Laguna) or checking out the caverns in **Nuevo Durango** (6 miles north of here).

Public transportation is almost nonexistent. In a car, you can reach Punta Laguna by turning southwest off Hwy 180 at Nuevo Xcan and driving 16 miles, or by heading 11 miles northeast from the Cobá junction.

GRAN CENOTE *Water Sports*

admission M$100

Gran Cenote is a worthwhile stop on your way between Tulum and the Cobá ruins, especially if it's a hot day. You can snorkel among small fish and see underwater formations in the caverns here if you bring your own gear. About a mile east of Gran Cenote are the smaller cenotes **Zacil-Ha** (admission M$30) and **Aktún-Ha** (admission M$30).

OCHO TULUM

Water Sports, Yoga

☎ 984-140-78-70; www.mexicokantours.com

About 5 miles south of the T-Junction in the Zona Hotelera, this hotel offers daily yoga classes. Inquire here also for kiteboarding packages. Four-hour kiteboarding courses are M$3250, while M$7150 gets you 10 hours of instruction.

Iñaki Iturbe

Information and Training Coordinator for Flora, Fauna y Cultura projects at Xcacel-Xcacelito

Tips for traveling green Don't throw your trash out. Use biodegradable sunblock. Don't take anything – plants, corals, shells – from the beach; they are integral to the natural environment. **Visiting turtle nesting beaches like Xcacel-Xcacelito (p77) responsibly** Respect the local fauna, especially turtle nests, which you'll find throughout the Riviera Maya. That means no smoking, no lights and no flash photography, and you should only talk in hushed tones.

ZAZIL-KIN *Water Sports*

☎ 984-124-00-82; www.hotelstulum.com/zazilkin

The PADI-certified dive shop at this hotel north of the T-junction in the Zona Hotelera is a good bet for ocean dives.

SHOP

Tulum's main drag, Av Tulum, is lined with shops offering many items (hammocks, blankets, handicrafts) that you will see up and down the Quintana Roo coast. Prices drop dramatically – up to 50% – the further you go from the bus station.

MEXICAN ART GALLERY

Gallery

☎ 984-745-89-79; inf_art@hotmail.com; 9am-6pm Mon-Sat

Located at the Hotel El Crucero, this gallery features the brightly colored work of local artist Enrique Diaz, whose motto is to 'paint the colors of Tulum.' His art is vivid and fun, a variety of portraits and landscapes that seem vaguely Picassoesque.

EAT

Many of the hotels in the Zona Hotelera also have excellent restaurants.

CHARLIE'S

Traditional Mexican $$

☎ 984-871-25-73; Av Tulum; 7:30am-11pm Tue-Sun

An old standby with attractive conch-shell decor and a wall made of old glass bottles, Charlie's is near the bus station and offers you the choice of indoor or courtyard dining. The food is largely Mexican, with a selection of salads thrown in.

WORTH THE TRIP: MAYA RUINS AT COBÁ

Though not as large as some of the more famous ruins, **Cobá** (admission M$51, parking M$40; 8am-5pm;) is cool because you feel like you're in the *Raiders of the Lost Ark* flick. It's set deep in the jungle and many of the ruins have yet to be excavated. Walk along ancient *sacbé* pathways (stone-paved avenues; *sacbeob* is the plural in Maya), climb up vine-covered mounds and ascend to the top of Nohoch Mul for a spectacular view of the surrounding jungle. Cobá was settled much earlier than nearby Chichén Itzá and Tulum, and construction reached its peak between AD 800 and 1100. Archaeologists believe that this city once covered an area of 50 sq km and held a population of 40,000 Maya.

About 4 miles south of town on the road to Chan Chen, you'll find a series of three locally administered cenotes: **Choo-Ha**, **Tamcach-Ha** and **Multún-Ha**. It costs M$45 (one cenote), M$70 (two cenotes) and M$100 (all three cenotes).

THE BALL GAME

Probably all pre-Hispanic Mexican cultures played some version of the Mesoamerican ritual ball game, the world's first-ever team sport. The game varied from place to place and era to era, but had certain lasting features. Over 500 ball courts have survived at archaeological sites around Mexico and Central America. The game seems to have been played between two teams and its essence was to keep a rubber ball off the ground by flicking it with hips, thighs, knees or elbows. The vertical or sloping walls alongside the courts were most likely part of the playing area. The game had (at least sometimes) deep religious significance, serving as an oracle, with the result indicating which of two courses of action should be taken. Games could be followed by the sacrifice of one or more of the players – whether winners or losers, no one is sure.

EL MARIACHI

Traditional Mexican $

Av Tulum; 7am-3am

Popular with locals and tourists alike, this open-air spot delivers yummy slow-cooked pork enchiladas, fresh grilled fish and about every cut of meat you could imagine.

LA NAVE *Italian* $$

984-871-25-92; Av Tulum; closed Sun

Perched over Av Tulum, this open-air Italian joint is perpetually packed. There's delicious pasta dishes – who doesn't love a bit of authentic *spaghetti amatriciana*? – plus there's crispy stone-fired pizzas and an assortment of continental meat and fish dishes on offer.

POSADA MARGHERITA

Italian $$$

984-801-84-93; www.posadamargherita.com; Km 4.5 Zona Hotelera

This Zona Hotelera hotel's restaurant is candlelit at night, making it a beautiful, romantic place to dine. The fantastic food, including the pasta, is made fresh daily and the wines are excellent.

SALSALITO TACO SHOP

Traditional Mexican $

Orión

Far enough removed from the main strip that you won't be sucking

YUCATÁN FAST FACTS

In living color Maya pyramids were painted in brilliant red, green, yellow and white colors. And the people of the region often painted their bodies red.

That's one big jungle The Selva Norte, which spans the southern part of the Yucatán Peninsula and northern Guatemala and Belize, is the world's second-largest tropical forest after the Amazon.

Underworlds Around 3000 cenotes (natural underground pools) dot the Yucatán Peninsula.

exhaust fumes, this *palapa*-thatched eatery has great fish and shrimp tacos, prepared just the way we like them with loads of cabbage and freshly chopped carrots on top. The fresh chips with just a hint of lime are the best in all of Quintana Roo.

WORTH THE TRIP: SIAN KA'AN BIOSPHERE RESERVE

Punta Allen sits at the end of a narrow spit of land that stretches south nearly 25 miles from its start below Tulum. There are some charming beaches along the way, with plenty of privacy, and most of the spit is within the protected, wildlife-rich **Sian Ka'an Biosphere Reserve** (Reserva de la Biosfera Sian Ka'an).

Sian Ka'an (meaning 'where the sky begins') is home to howler monkeys, anteaters, foxes, ocelots, pumas, crocodiles, eagles, raccoons, tapirs, peccaries, giant land crabs, jaguars and hundreds of bird species, including *chocolateras* (roseate spoonbills) and some flamingos.

There's an **entrance gate** to the reserve about 6 miles south of Tulum. Entrance is M$23. At the gate, there's a short nature trail taking you to a rather nondescript cenote (Ben Ha). The trail's short, so go ahead and take a second to have a gander.

Entering the reserve by land on the road to Punta Allen, you pass **Boca Paila Camps** (☎ 984-871-24-99; www.cesiak.org), where you can stop by to see the turtle rescue (M$325) or rent a kayak (M$425). If you'd prefer a guided tour, you can do that, too: a guided kayaking tour costs M$910; boating, M$1000; birding, M$1000; and fly-fishing, M$5000.

About half a mile south of here is the **Sian Ka'an visitor center** (Centro de Visitantes Reserva de la Biosfera Sian Ka'an), where you'll find some natural-history exhibits along with a watchtower that provides tremendous bird's-eye views of the lagoon.

If you can get all the way to Punta Allen, three locals with training in English, natural history, interpretation and birding conduct bird-watching, snorkeling and nature tours, mostly by boat, for about M$1500 for five to six people: **Marcos Nery** (marcosnatureguide@hotmail.com), **Baltazar Madera** (ask in Punta Allen) and **Chary Salazar** (inquire in Punta Allen at her restaurant of the same name).

There's also a fishing outfit just north of Punta Allen called **Pesca Maya** (☎ 998-883-42-04; www.pescamaya.com; 5am-10pm), which does daily saltwater fly-fishing runs and has a restaurant for guests only. **Vigía Grande** and **Galletanes** are among several of the Punta Allen's dining choices, both close to the water and both owned by co-ops. They serve Mexican dishes and seafood, including lobster. Neither has a phone and opening hours vary based on whether there are any customers.

The best way to reach Punta Allen by public transportation is by **colectivo** (☎ 984-115-55-80; M$200) out of Tulum: one leaves daily from Tulum center at 2pm and arrives about three hours later. Driving in a rental car is another option, but prepare for 5mph to 10mph speeds and more than a few transmission-grinding bumps.

BODY ARTISTS: CRANIAL DEFORMATION, PIERCING & TATTOOS

Take a second to imagine what a Maya at the height of the Classic period must have looked like. Their heads were sloped back, their ears, noses, cheeks and sometimes even genitals were pierced. Their eyes were crossed and their bodies were tattooed. These were, indeed, some of the first body artists.

Cranial deformation was one of the Maya's oddest forms of body art and was most often performed to indicate social status. Mothers would tightly bind the head of their infant (male or female) to a board while the skull was still soft. By positioning the board either on top of or behind the head, the mother could shape the skull in many ways – either long and pointy (known as 'elongated' – think *Coneheads*) or long and narrow, extending back rather than up (known as 'oblique' – think *Alien*). As the infant grew older and the bones calcified, the board was no longer needed: the skull would retain its modified shape for life. Apparently, compressing the skull did not affect the intelligence or capabilities of the child. The practice became less and less common after the Spanish arrived.

DRINK

CARIBE SWING *Bar*

Av Tulum

This is a locals' watering hole. It's generally a boys-only club and there are a few seats outside away from the blaring music.

PLAY

Tulum's nightlife is relatively subdued and most people just end up drinking at their hotel's bar. Stroll down Av Tulum to see where the action is.

DIVINO PARAÍSO *Dance Club*

Av Tulum

This happening rooftop bar is good for all you sinners and saints out there. We think Dante would approve. Come Tuesday nights for free salsa lessons.

>COSTA MAYA

Whether you're going by rental car or staring out a bus window, you'll notice the landscape changing as you head south from Tulum: the trees get taller and the birds more colorful along the beautiful stretch of cerulean sea known as the Costa Maya.

The *muy tranquilo* (very tranquil) coastal towns of Xcalak and Mahahual offer access to great birding, diving and snorkeling along this relatively pristine stretch of coast. Beautiful Laguna Bacalar provides fine escapes for people looking to get away from it all. And in the interior, the seldom-visited ruins of Dzibanché and Kohunlich seem all the more mysterious without the tour vans. Go in the early morning and you'll likely share the spot with vultures, leaf-cutter ants, mist and possibly an agouti or two. This rustic strip of the Quintana Roo coast is not for everyone, but for those seeking peace and a bit of solitude, it may be just what the doctor ordered.

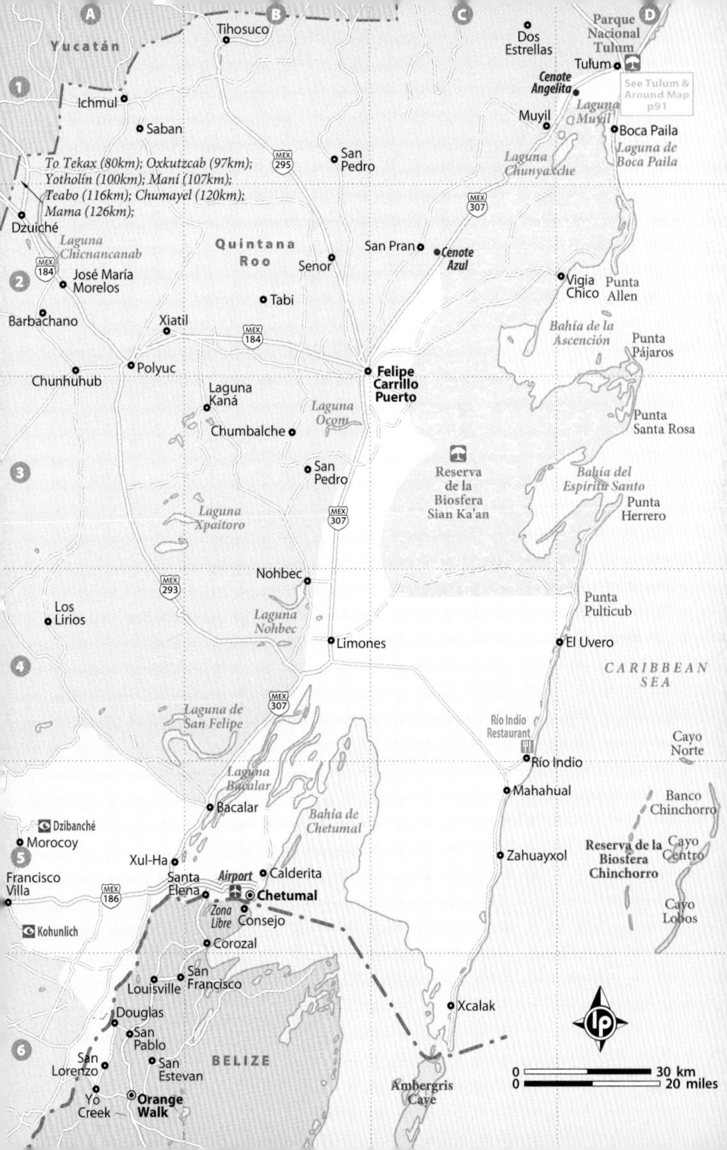

A
B
C
D
1
2
3
4
5
6
Yucatán
Tihosuco
Dos Estrellas
Parque Nacional Tulum
Tulum
See Tulum & Around Map p91
Cenote Angelita
Laguna Muyil
Muyil
Boca Paila
Laguna de Boca Paila
Laguna Chunyaxche
Ichmul
Saban
San Pedro
MEX 295
To Tekax (80km); Oxkutzcab (97km); Yotholín (100km); Maní (107km); Teabo (116km); Chumayel (120km); Mama (126km);
Dzuiché
Laguna Chicnancanab
MEX 184
José María Morelos
Quintana Roo
Senor
San Pran
Cenote Azul
MEX 307
Vigia Chico
Punta Allen
Tabi
Barbachano
Xiatil
Bahía de la Ascención
Punta Pájaros
Chunhuhub
Polyuc
Felipe Carrillo Puerto
Laguna Kaná
Laguna Ocom
Chumbalche
Punta Santa Rosa
San Pedro
Reserva de la Biosfera Sian Ka'an
Bahía del Espíritu Santo
Punta Herrero
Laguna Xpaitoro
Nohbec
MEX 293
Los Lirios
Laguna Nohbec
Punta Pulticub
Limones
El Uvero
CARIBBEAN SEA
Laguna de San Felipe
Río Indio Restaurant
Río Indio
Cayo Norte
Laguna Bacalar
Mahahual
Banco Chinchorro
Bacalar
Bahía de Chetumal
Dzibanché
Morocoy
Reserva de la Biosfera Chinchorro
Cayo Centro
Zahuayxol
Xul-Ha
Francisco Villa
MEX 186
Santa Elena
Airport
Calderita
Chetumal
Zona Libre
Consejo
Cayo Lobos
Kohunlich
Corozal
San Francisco
Louisville
Xcalak
Douglas
San Pablo
San Lorenzo
San Estevan
BELIZE
Yo Creek
Orange Walk
Ambergris Caye
0 30 km
0 20 miles

MAHAHUAL

With a brand new cruise-ship dock and *malecón* (beachfront pedestrian walk), Mahahual is looking good, especially considering that the small Costa Maya resort was virtually razed by Hurricane Dean in 2007.

Although the cruise-ship dock (just north of town) will eventually bring in ticky-tacky tourism shops and attractions, this small town retains for now a pretty laid-back Caribbean vibe, with most of the action happening on or near the new *malecón*. There's great diving and snorkeling, plus sugary white beaches that seem to go on forever.

GETTING THERE & AWAY

Mahahual is 80 miles south of Felipe Carrillo Puerto and approximately 60 miles northeast of Bacalar. A new ADO (p148) bus terminal, located next to the Hotel Mahahual just a block inland from the *malecón* (beachfront pedestrian walk), has made getting here easier than ever, though the buses are infrequent. They depart daily for Chetumal (M$88, 2½ hours, 6:30pm), Cancún (M$206, five hours, 10am), Felipe Carrillo Puerto (M$60, two hours, 10am), Laguna Bacalar (M$60, two hours, 6:30pm) and Tulum (M$132, four hours, 10am). There's a Pemex gas station in Mahahual if you need to fill your tank.

To get to Xcalak, you'll need to take a cab from Limones for about M$600. ADO buses to Chetumal (and Limones) leave at 5am and 2pm and cost M$70; the bus stops by the lighthouse.

SEE

MALECÓN

The beach right off Mahahual's beautiful *malecón* has great sand, plus water so shallow you can swim out a good 300ft. This is also where you'll find most of the town's best drinking spots and restaurants.

ZAHUAYXOL

Almost halfway between Mahahual and Xcalak you'll find this cute little beach, where sitting and watching the tides roll by is more of a passion than a pastime.

DO

BANCO CHINCHORRO

Water Sports

Divers won't want to miss the reefs and underwater fantasy worlds of the Banco Chinchorro, the largest coral atoll in the northern hemisphere. Some 30 miles long and up to 9 miles wide, Chinchorro's western edge lies about 20 miles off the coast and dozens of ships have fallen victim to its barely submerged ring of coral. The atoll and its surrounding waters were made a biosphere reserve (Reserva de

WORTH THE TRIP: FELIPE CARRILLO PUERTO

Those traveling to the Costa Maya by land will likely pass through the small town of Felipe Carrillo Puerto. This predominantly Maya town is a must-see for any history buff in your crew, having played a key role in the War of the Castes.

In 1849, when the War of the Castes turned against them, the Maya of the northern Yucatán Peninsula made their way to this town seeking refuge. Regrouping, they were ready to sally forth again in 1850 when a 'miracle' occurred. A wooden cross erected at a cenote on the western edge of the town began to 'talk,' telling the Maya they were the chosen people, exhorting them to continue the struggle against the Spanish and promising victory. The talking was actually done by a ventriloquist who used sound chambers, but the people looked upon it as the authentic voice of their aspirations. You can visit the cross today at the **Santuario de la Cruz Parlante** (Sanctuary of the Talking Cross), about five blocks west of the gas station on Hwy 307.

la Biosfera Banco Chinchorro) to protect them from depredation.

DREAMTIME DIVE CENTER *Water Sports*

☎ 983-700-58-24; www.dreamtimediving.com

This well-run establishment, located 1.7 miles south of the military checkpoint, has trips to stretches of the barrier reef and offers PADI courses. Most dives go to a maximum of 100ft, as there are no decompression chambers for miles. And with a ban on wreck dives recently lifted, there are plenty of shipwreck sites worth exploring. Along the way you'll also spot coral walls and canyons, rays, turtles, giant sponges, grouper, tangs, eels and, in some spots, reef, tiger and hammerhead sharks.

FISHING *Water Sports*

Local tour operators arrange fishing trips (M$600 per hour for up to four people). Look for signs along the *malecón*.

LAS CABAÑAS DEL DOCTOR *Water Sports*

☎ 983-107-51-26; www.lascabanasdeldoctor.com

Located a mile south of the military checkpoint, the doctor – he's not a real doctor; he just plays one on TV – rents canoes for M$100 an hour.

NATIVE CHOICE *Tours*

cell phone ☎ 983-1020532; www.thenativechoice.com

This excellent outfit offers guided tours to interesting places inland from Mahahual. Led by the animated English-speaking guide David Villagómez, these tours take you to unexcavated Maya ruins at the Parque Natural Lagarteras, forgotten churches along the **Ruta de los Conventos** near Tihosuco and maybe even across the Laguna Chicnancanab in a kayak. Ask him about tours to the Ichkabal Maya site, which may be open to the public by 2012.

SNORKELING *Water Sports*

There's good snorkeling at Banco Chinchorro, including **40 Cannons**, a wooden ship in 15ft to 20ft of water. Looters have taken all but about 25 of the cannons and it can only be visited in ideal conditions. There's also good snorkeling right off Mahahual's *malecón*, or you can ask a local fisherman here to take you out for about M$200 per hour.

YUCATÁN FAST FACTS

Think before you drink! Around 2.7 million tons of plastic are used to bottle water each year worldwide. Stay green by asking your hotelier to provide water coolers or by carrying your own water filter.

Mamá's cooking A regular Monday dish in most Yucatecan homes is *frijol con puerco,* a Yucatecan version of pork and beans. Pork cooked with black beans is served with rice and garnished with radish, cilantro (coriander) and onions.

Spicy peppers The strongest demand for habanero chili grown in Yucatán comes from Japan. Japanese companies normally buy the chili in its powdered form and add it to a wide variety of spicy snacks.

MIND YOUR MANNERS

Some indigenous people adopt a cool attitude toward visitors: they have come to mistrust outsiders after five centuries of rough treatment. Just like anyone else, they don't like being gawked at by tourists and can be very sensitive about cameras. Ask first if you have any doubt at all about whether it's OK to take a photo.

SHOP

ARTISAN MARKET *Market*

On the northern section of the *malecón*, you'll find a decent artisan market. Given that this region was only inhabited by fisherman just a few decades ago, there are no handicrafts that are truly original to the area, but the wood carvings and blankets are nice gifts for the folks back home nonetheless.

EAT

There are about a dozen restaurants along the *malecón*, each offering the standard assortment of seafood, Mexican favorites and pub grub.

100% AGAVE

Traditional Mexican $

Cien Por Ciento Agave; 11am-late

Located just a bit north of the soccer field one block inland from the *malecón*, this restaurant-bar offers up delicious tacos, a chillaxed locals' vibe and the best margaritas this side of the Río Bravo del Norte.

MAYA BAR *Seafood* $$

9am-10pm

On the northern end of the *malecón*, this friendly family place specializes in ceviche and seafood cocktails. There's also a swing bar for the swinger in all of us.

POSADA DE LOS 40 CAÑONES *Italian* $$

983-125-85-91; www.40canones.com

This Italian-owned restaurant and hotel, on the *malecón* a mile south of the military checkpoint, is clean and comfortable. The open-air restaurant has good Italian eats, plus international favorites like burgers and quesadillas.

RÍO INDIO RESTAURANT *Seafood* $

This little ceviche and *cerveza* (beer) shack, 5 miles north of town on the road to El Uvero, basically has the beach all to itself. While you'll need to hop in the car to get here, it makes for a fun afternoon excursion.

DRINK

Cruise along the *malecón* for swing bars and low-key lounges. 100% Agave, opposite, is one of our favorites.

TINY TRAILBLAZERS

The small trails you'll see crisscrossing the cleared areas in many of the ruins baffle observant visitors. What made them? A rodent? To get the answer right you have to think tiny: ants. Leaf-cutter ants, to be specific. Sometimes marching up to a mile or more from their colony, leaf-cutter ants walk in single file along predetermined routes, often wearing down a pathway over a period of months or years. Patient observers can often see the tiny landscapers at work, carrying fingernail-sized clippings back home. Though they can bite if disturbed, these ants are generally harmless and should be left in peace to do their work.

XCALAK

The rickety wooden houses, beached fishing launches and lazy gliding pelicans make this tiny town plopped in the middle of nowhere a perfect escape. Despite its proximity to Hurricane Dean's ground zero in Mahahual, Xcalak (ish-kah-*lak*) escaped the brunt of the storm. And blessed by virtue of its remoteness and the Chinchorro barrier reef (preventing the creation of a cruise-ship port), Xcalak may yet escape the development boom.

STOCK UP BEFORE YOU VISIT

Xcalak is seeing negative population growth. Specializing in coconuts, it was an important port during the War of the Castes and the town even had a cinema until a series of hurricanes wiped everything away. Today, there are no signs of it getting a bank, grocery store or gas station anytime soon, so stock up before you come.

There's great diving at the barrier reef, but if diving isn't your thing, there's still plenty to do. Come here to walk in dusty streets and sip frozen drinks while frigates soar above translucent-green lagoons. Explore a mangrove swamp by kayak or just doze in a hammock and soak up some sun.

SEE

MAYA RUIN

There's a remote and seldom-visited Maya ruin on the west side of the lagoon. Ask your hotelier to arrange a tour.

DO

KAYAKING *Water Sports*

The mangrove swamps stretching inland from the coastal road hide some large lagoons and form tunnels that invite kayakers to explore. They and the drier forest teem with wildlife: as well as the usual herons,

Be touched by a shaft of light as you cruise across the cerulean pool of Cenote Azul

PASCALE BEROUJON

WORTH THE TRIP: SOUTHERN QUINTANA ROO

Intrepid explorers should consider traveling from the Costa Maya for the following day trips.

Bio Maya (☎ 983-132-21-22; Carretera Cancún–Chetumal Km 32.5; admission adult/child M$578/498) Offers a heart-pumping zip-line ride. . . yippee!

Cenote Azul Just shy of the south end of the *costera* is Cenote Azul, a 300ft-deep natural pool on the southwest shore of the lake. There's a nice bar and hotel here. It's 600ft east of Hwy 307, so many buses will drop you nearby.

Dzibanché and Kohunlich Also reachable as a long day trip from Mahahual, the sites of Dzibanché and Kohunlich make up the Corredor Arqueológico (archaeological corridor). About 12 miles northeast of Dzibanché is the Preclassic site of Ichkabal. This site, considered by many to be a predecessor to Calakmul, is slated to open sometime in 2011 or 2012.

Laguna Bacalar This beautiful lake comes as a surprise in a region of tortured limestone and scrubby jungle. More than 25 miles long with a bottom of sparkling white sand, this adventure spot offers opportunities for camping, swimming, kayaking, bird-watching and simply lazing around.

Ruta de los Conventos This long day trip from Mahahual takes you to colonial-era convents in the towns of Maní, Oxkutzcab, Teabo, Mama, Chumayel, Tekax and Yotholín.

egrets and other waterfowl, you can see agouti, jabiru (storks), iguanas, javelinas (peccaries), parakeets, kingfishers, alligators and more. Unfortunately, the mangrove also breeds mosquitoes and some vicious *jejenes* (sand flies).

XTC DIVE CENTER

Water Sports

www.xtcdivecenter.com

This shop, a quarter mile north of town on the coast road, offers dive and snorkel trips (from M$390) to the wondrous barrier reef just offshore, and to Banco Chinchorro (three-tank dive M$2470). It also rents diving equipment, offers PADI open-water certificates for M$5655, and arranges fishing and birding tours. You can get your M$50 national park wristband to visit Chinchorro here or at the park office in town.

 EAT

Many restaurants close during low season, May through November.

LEAKY PALAPA

Contemporary $$

5-10pm Fri-Mon, closed low season

Chef Marla and partner Linda have turned an old standby three blocks west of the plaza into a new sensation, serving wonderful meals such as lobster in caramel ginger sauce. Opinion was unanimous that this was the best place to go to treat your taste buds.

LONCHERÍA SILVIA'S

Seafood $

9am-10pm

Located three blocks south of the plaza a block in from the coast, Silvia's serves mostly fish fillets and ceviche, and keeps pretty regular hours. The long menu doesn't mean that everything is available. You'll likely end up having the fish.

DRINK

XCALAK CARIBE *Bar*

noon-late

This classic Caribbean watering hole three blocks north of the plaza on the beach – complete with a bar fashioned from an old ship's hull – is your best bet for nightlife in town.

>EXPLORE THE YUCATÁN

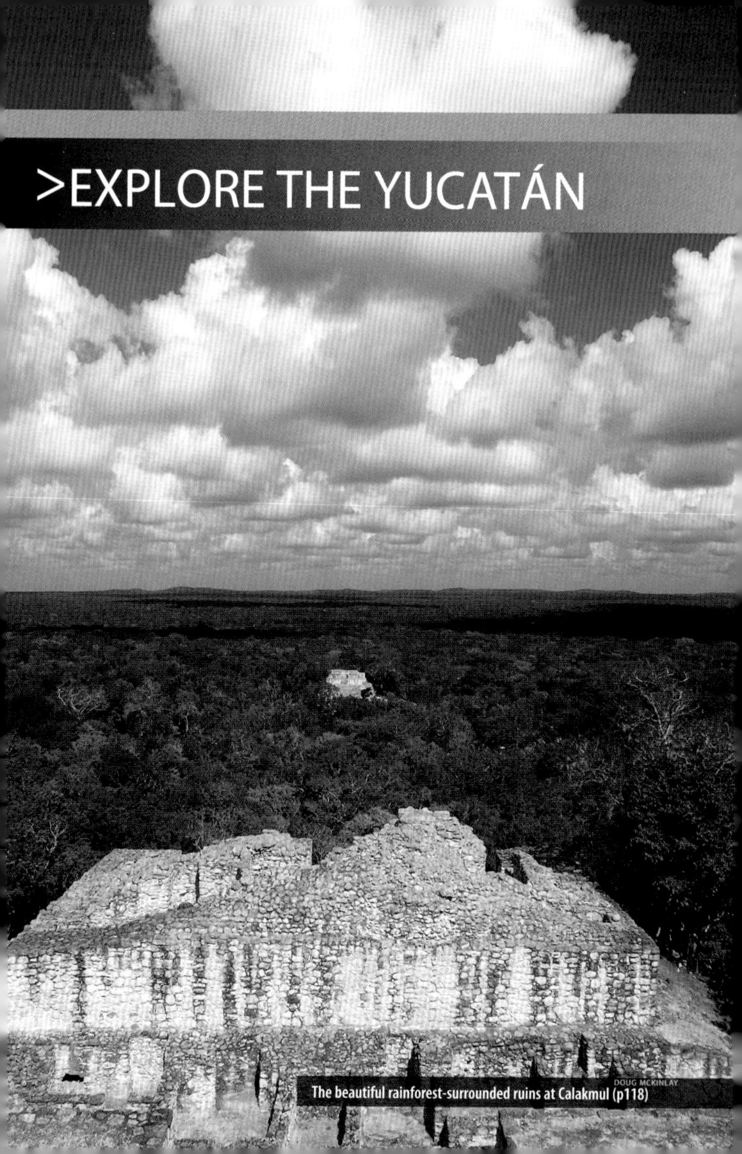

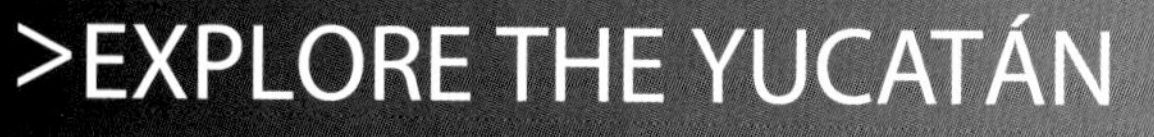

DOUG MCKINLAY

The beautiful rainforest-surrounded ruins at Calakmul (p118)

>CHICHÉN ITZÁ

The most famous and best restored of the Yucatán Maya sites, **Chichén Itzá** (Mouth of the Well of the Itzáes; admission M$111, parking M$20, sound-&-light show M$40, guide M$500-600; 8am-6pm summer, to 5:30pm winter), while tremendously overcrowded – every gaper and his grandmother are trying to check off the new seven wonders of the world – will still impress even the most jaded visitor.

Most archaeologists agree that the first major settlement at Chichén Itzá, late in the Classic period, was pure Maya. In about the 9th century, the city was largely abandoned for reasons unknown. It was resettled around the late 10th century and shortly thereafter it is believed to have been invaded by the Toltecs, who had migrated from their central highlands capital of Tula, north of Mexico City. The bellicose Toltec culture was fused with that of the Maya, incorporating the cult of Quetzalcóatl (Kukulcán in Maya).

The visitors center has a small but worthwhile **museum** (8am-5pm). As you approach from the visitors center into the site, **El Castillo** (also called the Pyramid of Kukulcán) rises before you in all its grandeur. Nearby, the **great ball court**, the largest and most impressive in Mexico, is only one of the city's eight courts, indicative of the importance of the games held here. The structure at the northern end of the ball court, called the **Temple of the Bearded Man** after a carving inside it, has some finely sculpted pillars and reliefs of flowers, birds and trees. The **Temple of the Jaguars and Shields**, built atop the southeast corner of the great ball court's wall, has some columns with carved rattlesnakes and tablets with etched jaguars. The **Platform of Skulls** (*tzompantli* in Náhuatl) is between the Temple of the Jaguars and Shields and El Castillo. You can't mistake it, because the T-shaped platform is festooned with carved skulls and eagles tearing open the chests of men to eat their hearts. About 2 miles southeast of the eastern entrance to the ruins is **Ik Kil Parque Ecoarqueológico** (985-858-15-25;

INFORMATION

Getting there Daily buses and tours take you to the site from Cancún (M$108, 4½ hours), Tulum (M$101, three hours) and everywhere in between; see www.ticketbus.com.mx.

Accommodations Those on a budget should check out the Pirámide Inn (985-851-01-15; www.chichen.com; Calle 15A No 30; hammock or tent site per person M$50, r M$450;), while Hotel Mayaland (998-887-24-95, in the USA 800-235-4079; www.mayaland.com; d/ste M$2500/3700;) offers upscale digs.

Further info www.chichenitza.com

adult/child M$70/35; 8am-6pm), the cenote of which has been developed into a divine swimming spot. The otherworldly caves at the **Grutas de Balankanché** (adult.under 12yr M$67/free; ticket booth 9am-5pm Mon-Sat) are located 3 miles east of the ruins of Chichén Itzá, on the highway to Cancún.

>VALLADOLID

Also known as the Sultaness of the East, Yucatán's third-largest city is known for its quiet streets and sun-splashed, pastel walls. She certainly is one sultry babe, and it's worth staying here for at least a few hours on your way to Chichén Itzá.

Valladolid has seen its fair share of turmoil and revolt over the years. The city was first founded in 1543 near the Chouac-Ha lagoon some 30 miles from the coast, but it was too hot and there were way too many mosquitoes for Francisco de Montejo, nephew of Montejo the Elder, and his merry band of conquerors. So they upped and moved the city to the Maya ceremonial center of Zací (sah-*see*), where they faced heavy resistance from the local Maya. Eventually Montejo the Elder's son, Montejo the Younger, took the town.

During much of the colonial era, the Maya of the area suffered brutal exploitation, which continued after Mexican independence. Barred from entering many areas of the city, the Maya made Valladolid one of their first points of attack following the 1847 outbreak of the War of the Castes.

The **Templo de San Bernardino and Convento de Sisal** (8am-noon & 5-9pm) are about half a mile southwest of the plaza. They were constructed between 1552 and 1560 to serve the dual functions of fortress and church. The **Museo de San Roque** (Calle 41; admission free; 9am-9pm), between Calles 38 and

INFORMATION

Getting there Many tours to Chichén Itzá stop in Valladolid in the afternoon. Otherwise, grab a bus from Cancún (M$128, two hours), Tulum (M$70, two hours) or Playa del Carmen (M$120, 2½ hours).Check out www.ticketbus.com.mx for more bus info.

Accommodations Budget busters head to Hostel La Candelaria (cell phone 019-858562267; Calle 35 No 201F; dm/r without bathroom incl breakfast M$100/250;), while fancier digs can be had at Hotel San Clemente (985-856-31-61; www.hotelsanclemente.com.mx; Calle 42 No 206; s/d with fan M$375/425, with air-con M$398/448; P).

Further info www.yucatantoday.com/en/topics/valladolid

40, has models and exhibits relating the history of the city and the region. Other displays focus on various aspects of traditional Maya life.

Among the region's several underground cenotes is **Cenote Zací** (Calle 36; admission M$25; 8am-6pm), set in a park that also holds traditional stone-walled thatched houses and a small zoo. People swim in Zací, though being mostly open it has some dust and algae. Enter from Calle 39.

A bit more enticing but less accessible is **Cenote Dzitnup** (Xkekén; admission M$25; 8am-5pm), 4.5 miles west of the plaza. It's artificially lit and very swimmable, and a massive limestone formation dripping with stalactites hangs from its ceiling. Across the road about 300ft closer to town is **Cenote Samulá** (admission M$25; 8am-6pm), a lovely cavern pool with *álamo* roots stretching down many feet from the middle of the ceiling to drink from it.

On Calle 32 the **mercado municipal** is a good, authentic Mexican market, where locals come to shop for cheap clothing, home wares, meat and produce, and to eat at inexpensive *taquerías*.

>RÍO LAGARTOS

On the windy northern shore of the peninsula, sleepy Río Lagartos is a fishing village that also boasts the densest concentration of flamingos in Mexico, supposedly two or three flamingos per Mexican, if one believes the math. Lying within the **Reserva de la Biosfera Ría Lagartos**, this mangrove-lined estuary also shelters 334 other species of resident and migratory birds, including snowy egrets, red egrets, tiger herons and snowy white

INFORMATION

Getting there Several Noreste buses (p148) run daily between Río Lagartos and Tizimín (M$25, one hour), Mérida (M$130, three to four hours) and San Felipe (M$6, 20 minutes). Noreste and Mayab also serve Cancún (M$130, three to four hours) three times daily. See www.ticketbus.com.mx for further bus information.

En route On your way to Río Lagartos, be sure to check out the ruins at Ek' Balam (admission M$31, guide M$250; 8am-4:30pm). From the parking lot, you can check out the **X-Canché Cenote** (cell phone 985-1009915; admission M$30, bike rental M$70, bike, rappel & kayak tour M$200; 8am-5pm).

Accommodations For cheap sleeps, try Posada Isla Contoy (986-862-00-00; www.flyfishingyucatan.com; Calle 19 No 134; s/d M$250/350;) or the slightly more upscale Hotel Villas de Pescadores (986-862-00-20; villa_pescadores@prodigy.net.mx; cnr Calle 14 & Calle 9; d with fan/air-con M$400/500;).

Further info www.flyfishingyucatan.com

ibis, as well as a small number of the once-numerous crocodiles that gave the town its name.

To take a **flamingo tour**, you'll need to rent a boat and driver. You'll see more birdlife if you head out at sunrise or around 4pm. Prices vary by boat, group size (maximum six) and destination. A one-hour trip costs around M$500 and two to three hours is M$600. In addition, the reserve charges visitors a M$24 admission fee. Plan on packing something to eat the night before, as most restaurants open long after you'll be on the water. Ask to stop at the *arcilla* (mud bath) on the way back.

The best guides are to be found at **Restaurante-Bar Isla Contoy** (☎ 986-862-00-00); driving into town, turn left on Calle 19 at the sign for the restaurant-bar.

If time permits, seek out **Ismael Navarro** (☎ 986-862-00-00; Restaurante-Bar Isla Contoy) or **Diego Núñez Martínez** (diego2909@yahoo.com; La Torreja Restaurant), two licensed guides with formal training as naturalists. For M$200 you can get a boat to take you across the lagoon for a couple of hours on the beach.

Just 3 miles from the nearby fishing village of San Felipe, tiny **Isla Cerritos** was an important Maya port city back in the day. While the entire island was covered with buildings during this era – archaeological expeditions have turned up nearly 50,000 artifacts – it's virtually deserted today and none of the buildings have been restored. From Río Lagartos, you can take a half-day **snorkeling tour** of the island for M$800. From San Felipe, it'll run you between M$600 and M$700. Hire your boats on the waterfront of either town.

>IZAMAL

You'll need to take at least two days to head across to the seldom-visited city of Izamal, but the trip may just be worth it for serious cultural inquisitors.

In ancient times Izamal was a center for the worship of the supreme Maya god, Itzamná, and the sun god, Kinich-Kakmó. A dozen temple pyramids were devoted to these or other gods. No doubt these bold expressions of Maya religiosity are why the Spanish colonists chose Izamal as the site for an enormous and impressive Franciscan monastery, which still stands at the heart of this town, located about 40 miles east of Mérida.

The Izamal of today is a quiet provincial town, nicknamed La Ciudad Amarilla (The Yellow City) for the traditional yellow buildings that spiral out from the center like a budding daisy. It's easily explored on foot and

INFORMATION

Getting there Oriente operates frequent buses between Mérida and Izamal (M$20 to M$25, 1½ hours) from the Noreste bus terminal. There are also buses from Valladolid (M$44, two hours). Coming from Chichén Itzá, you must change buses at Hoctún. See www.ticketbus.com.mx for more bus info.
Accommodations The best hotel in town is Macan Ché (☎ 988-954-02-87; www.macanche.com; Calle 22 No 305; r with fan/air-con incl breakfast M$420/650;).
Further info www.yucatantoday.com/en/topics/izamal

horse-drawn carriages add to the city's charm. To best explore the city, stop by the **tourist center** (☎ 988-954-00-09; Palacio Municipal, Plaza Central) and ask for a copy of the multilingual tourist map.

When the Spaniards conquered Izamal, they destroyed the major Maya temple, the Ppapp-Hol-Chac pyramid, and in 1533 began to build from its stones one of the first monasteries in the western hemisphere. Work on **Convento de San Antonio de Padua** (admission free; 6am-8pm) was finished in 1561. Under the monastery's arcades, look for building stones with an unmistakable mazelike design; these were clearly taken from the earlier Maya temple.

The monastery's principal church is the **Santuario de la Virgen de Izamal**, approached by a ramp from the main square. The ramp leads into the **Atrium**, a huge arcaded courtyard in which the **Fiesta of the Virgin of Izamal** takes place each August 15. There's a **sound-and-light show** (admission M$40; 8:30pm Tue, Thu & Sat) three nights a week.

Southeast of the convent on the plaza is the small **Museo de los Grandes Maestros del Arte Mexicano** (Calle 31 No 201; admission M$20; 10am-8pm Mon-Sat, to 5pm Sun), an art museum and gallery showcasing pop art from around Mexico. It's also worth taking the time to visit the **talleres de arte** (artisan workshops) found throughout the city.

Three of the town's original 12 Maya **pyramids** have been partially restored. The largest (and the third largest in Yucatán) is the enormous **Kinich-Kakmó**, three blocks north of the monastery. You can climb it for free most of the time. If a guard is there, it's nice to make a M$20 donation.

Some 80 pre-Hispanic structures have been discovered within the city limits. **Habuk, Itzamatul** and **Chaltún Há** are just a few. Hire a guide at the tourist center to visit them.

>MÉRIDA & YUCATÁN STATE

Since the Spanish conquest, Mérida has been the cultural capital of the entire peninsula. At times provincial, at others *'muy cosmopolitano,'* it is a town steeped in colonial history, with narrow streets, broad central plazas and the region's best museums. It's also a perfect hub to kick off your adventure into the rest of Yucatán state and can easily be enjoyed on a short two- or three-day jaunt from Cancún. There are cheap eats, good hostels and hotels, thriving markets and goings-on just about every night somewhere in the downtown area.

The **Plaza Grande** is one of the nicest plazas in Mexico. On Sunday hundreds of *meridanos* take their *paseo* (stroll) here and there's a cultural exhibit – normally dance or live music – nearly every night.

On the plaza's east side, on the site of a former Maya temple, is Mérida's hulking, severe **Catedral de San Ildefonso** (6am-noon & 4-7pm), begun in 1561 and completed in 1598. Some of the stone from the Maya temple was used in its construction.

South of the cathedral, housed in the former archbishop's palace, is the **Museo de Arte Contemporáneo** (Macay; 999-928-32-36; Calle 60, btwn Calles 61 & 63; admission free; 10am-5:15pm Wed, Thu, Sun & Mon, to 7:15pm Fri & Sat). This attractive museum holds permanent exhibits of Yucatán's most famous painters and sculptors, as well as revolving exhibits by local craftspeople.

Across the square from the cathedral is Mérida's **Palacio Municipal** (City Hall). Originally built in 1542, it was twice refurbished, in the 1730s and the 1850s. Adjoining it is the **Centro Cultural Olimpio** (cnr Calles 62 & 61), Mérida's municipal cultural center.

INFORMATION

Getting there There are frequent 1st- and 2nd-class buses between Mérida and Cancún (M$179 to M$418, four to six hours); see www.ticketbus.com.mx.

Accommodations Hostel goers should check out Nómadas Youth Hostel (999-924-52-23; www.nomadastravel.com; Calle 62 No 433; dm M$109, s/d without bathroom M$199/268, d with bathroom M$328; P). For upscale, gay-friendly digs, head to Los Arcos Bed & Breakfast (999-928-02-14; www.losarcosmerida.com; Calle 66, btwn Calles 49 & 53; s/d M$850/950;).

Further info www.yucatantoday.com

FOUR AMAZING DAY TRIPS FROM MÉRIDA

If you have an extra day to explore, here are some worthwhile day trips from the capital:

Celestún Head out early to catch a mangrove birding tour. It's about M$250 per person, including the boat trip.

Cuzamá Three amazing cenotes accessed by horse-drawn cart. The cost for a group of four is around M$200.

Dzibilchaltún & Progreso Visit the ruins and cenote for about M$80 or extend your trip for an afternoon of beach time in Progreso.

Ruta Puuc Ruin yourself by visiting all five sites (including megadraw Uxmal) in one day. The trip lasts about eight hours and costs around M$350 per person.

A half-dozen blocks away, the **city museum** (☎ 999-923-68-69; Calle 56, btwn Calles 65 & 67; admission free; 🕒 9am-8pm Tue-Fri, to 2pm Sat & Sun) is housed in the old post office and offers a great reprieve from the hustle, honks and exhaust of this market neighborhood. Another popular museum is the **Museo de Arte Popular de Yucatán** (Yucatecan Museum of Popular Art; Casa Molina, cnr Calles 50A & 57; admission M$20, free Sunday; 🕒 9:30am-6pm Tue-Sat, 9am-2pm Sun), which is six blocks east of the Plaza Grande in an edifice built in 1906. There's a small rotating exhibit downstairs that features pop art from around Mexico.

The **city tourist office** (☎ 999-942-00-00, ext 80119; Calle 62 on Plaza Grande) offers free daily guided walking tours of the historic center (sometimes in English), focusing on Plaza Grande. Tours depart at 9.30am from in front of the Palacio Municipal.

>ISLA HOLBOX

Isn't life great when it's lo-fi and low-rise? That's the attitude on friendly Isla Holbox (hol-bosh), with its sandy streets, colorful Caribbean buildings and lazing, sun-drunk dogs. There's so little to do here, in fact, that even the bars close at 8pm or 9pm (at least during low season). Holbox is thus a welcome refuge for anyone looking to just get away from it all ('all' likely meaning the hubbub of Cancún!). It's nearly impossible to take a day trip here from Cancún unless you've got your own wheels – and even that would be a push – so we'd suggest instead an investment of two or three days for a nice relaxing weekend trip.

The island is about 18 miles long and from a third of a mile to a mile wide, with seemingly endless beaches, tranquil waters and a galaxy of shells in various shapes and colors. Lying within the **Yum Balam Reserve**,

Holbox is home to more than 150 species of bird, including roseate spoonbills, pelicans, herons, ibis and flamingos. The waters are abundant with fish, and dolphins can be seen year-round. In summer, whale sharks congregate relatively nearby in unheard-of quantities. **Willy's Tours** (☎ 984-875-20-08; holbox@hotmail.com; Av Tiburón Ballena), near Mini Súper Besa, offers whale-shark tours (M$900 per person). Ask to stop for a quick snorkel on the way back from your trip – the guides will normally agree to this. Strong northerly winds could make for great kiteboarding and windsurfing, though you'll need to bring your own kit.

The water is not the translucent turquoise common to Quintana Roo beach sites, because here the Caribbean mingles with the darker Gulf of Mexico. The island's dark-water lagoon on the south side inspired the Maya to name it Holbox, meaning 'black hole.' During the rainy season (May through September) there are clouds of mosquitoes: bring repellent and be prepared to stay inside for a couple of hours after dusk.

Many hotels will book tours of the area's attractions. To get around the island, consider renting a rusty beach-cruiser bicycle from **Artesanias La Isla** on the plaza for M$15 per hour or M$100 per day.

On the western edge of the island, about a mile and a half from downtown, **Punta Coco** is a great sunset beach. On the eastern side, you have **Punta Mosquito** about a mile and a half east from the downtown area. It has a large sandbar and is a good spot to sight flamingos. Golf-cart taxis will take you to either spot for M$80.

INFORMATION

Getting there A *barco* (boat) ferries passengers (M$60, 25 minutes) to Holbox from the port village of Chiquilá nine times daily from 5am to 6pm in winter, 6am to 7pm in summer. Two Mayab buses leave Cancún daily for Chiquilá (M$75, 3½ hours) at 7:50am and 12:40pm. There's also an Oriente bus from Valladolid (M$78, 2½ hours) at 2:45am. See www.ticketbus.com.mx for more bus info.

En route Check out Puerta Verde (www.puertaverde.com.mx) for info on grassroots tourist development in the towns of Solferino and San Ángel, easy stops on your way to Chiquilá if you're driving a car.

Accommodations Take a golf-cart taxi to Hostel Ida y Vuelta (☎ 984-875-23-58; www.camping-mexico.com/home_uk.htm; camping M$80, hammock M$90, dm M$100, r M$550, bungalow M$600;) or spend big at Casa Sandra (☎ 984-875-21-71; www.casasandra.com; r incl breakfast M$1860-4810, villa incl breakfast M$7735;).

Further info www.holboxisland.com

>CALAKMUL

If you're totally into Maya history – or nature reserves – you might consider a three- to five-day expedition into the Campeche countryside to the Maya ruins of **Calakmul** (☎ 555-150-20-73; admission M$41, road maintenance fee per car M$40, local tax per person M$40; 8am-4:30pm). The site was 'discovered' in 1931 by American botanist Cyrus Lundell and bears comparison in size and historical significance to Tikal in Guatemala, its chief rival for hegemony over the southern lowlands during the Classic era.

A central chunk of its 28-sq-mile expanse has been consolidated and partially restored but, owing to ecological considerations, clearing has been kept to a minimum. Most of the city's approximately 7200 remnants lie covered in jungle; exploration and restoration are ongoing. You can get a Calakmul map online at http://mayaruins.com/calakmul/calakmul_map.html.

Visiting Calakmul is as much an ecological experience as a historical one. Lying at the heart of the vast, untrammeled **Reserva de la Biosfera Calakmul** (which covers close to 15% of the state's total territory), the ruins are surrounded by rainforest, with cedar, mahogany, sapodilla and rubber trees dotting a seemingly endless canopy of vegetation. While wandering amid the ruins, you may glimpse wild turkeys, parrots and toucans among the roughly 230 bird species that reside or fly through here. You may also come across peccaries, agoutis or howler monkeys, as well as numerous lizards and snakes. Five of the six wildcats found in Mexico inhabit the reserve, including the sacred jaguar. The earlier in the day you come, the more wildlife you're likely to spot.

En route to the site, stop in the dusty truckers town of Xpujil to mount adventures to the neighboring ruins of **Balamkú**, **Becán**, **Chicanná**, **Río Bec**, **Xpujil** and **Hormiguero**.

INFORMATION

Getting there Calakmul and the other neighboring sites are best accessed from Xpujil. There's one ADO bus (p148) at 10:35am from Cancún (M$243 to M$324, 6½ hours) and two ADO buses and two Sur buses from Chetumal (M$102, 1½ hours); see www.ticketbus.com.mx.
Accommodations Try Río Bec Dreams (opposite) or the more upscale Hotel Puerta Calakmul (☎ 998-892-26-42; www.puertacalakmul.com.mx; cabañas low/high season M$1430/1560;) for lodging near Calakmul.
Further info www.campeche.travel

Around 600ft east of the Xpujil junction, **Servidores Turísticos Calakmul** (☎ 983-871-60-64; ciitcalakmul@prodigy.net.mx; Carretera Escárcega-Chetumal Km 153; 9am-2pm & 3-7pm Mon-Sat) provides ecotours led by trained guides from nearby communities. On one popular excursion you can observe millions of bats emerging from a cenote. One-day tours to Calakmul for up to 12 people cost M$900. It also rents bikes for M$150 a day.

Río Bec Dreams (www.riobecdreams.com; Hwy 186 Km 142; cabañas with/without bathroom M$800/420) provides unquestionably the best accommodations in the area. Enthusiastic and knowledgeable promoters of the zone, owners Rick and Diane also conduct highly recommended tours of Calakmul, Río Bec and other sites in the area. Look for the flags on the north side of the highway a mile west of Chicanná.

>SNAPSHOTS

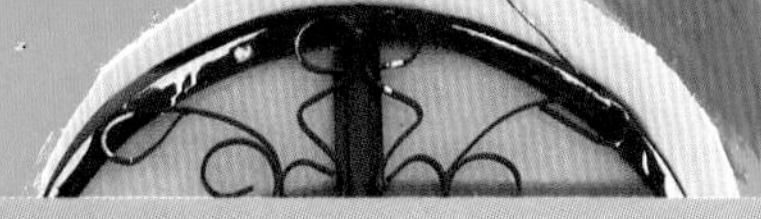

This is Mexico's number one destination...and with good reason. Sun worshippers love the peroxide-blonde beaches, while the shimmering waters are perfect for diving and snorkeling enthusiasts. There're Maya ruins for cultural explorers, energized nightclubs for bon vivants and excellent food and lodging for everyday epicures.

GUYLAIN DOYLE

The turquoise of Quintana Roo's coast is echoed in this house exterior

>ACCOMMODATIONS

Accommodations in the Yucatán range from simple hammocks and *cabañas* (cabins) to world-class luxury resorts. Cancún and the Riviera Maya are home to the largest all-inclusive resorts in the area. In Isla Mujeres, Playa del Carmen and Tulum, you can expect funked-out boutique hotels – though you are less likely to have an ocean view, these unique offerings are probably right for you if cattle calls and bikini contests are not your thing. In places like Cozumel, the Costa Maya and the small towns along the Riviera Maya, like Akumal and Tankah, home rentals rule supreme.

Budget accommodations (M$100 to M$550) include campgrounds, hammocks, palm-thatched *cabañas,* backpacker hostels, guesthouses and cheaper hotels. Accommodations will be without frills but generally clean. Hotel rooms, even in the budget range, usually have a private bathroom containing hot shower, toilet and washbasin.

Midrange accommodations (M$550 to M$1200) are chiefly hotels. In some areas of the Yucatán M$550 can get you a cozy, attractively decorated room in a friendly small hotel. Many of the region's most appealing and memorable lodgings are in the midrange bracket – small or medium-sized hotels, well cared for, with a friendly atmosphere and personal attention from staff. In some areas you'll also find apartments, bungalows and more comfortable *cabañas* in this price range.

Top-end hotels (M$1200 and up) run from classy international hotels in cities to deluxe coastal resorts and luxurious smaller establishments catering to travelers with a taste for comfort and beautiful design, and the funds to pay for them.

Fortunately for families and small groups of travelers, many hotels in all price ranges have rooms for three, four or five people that cost not much more than a double.

In the Yucatán, high season runs from Christmas right through to Easter, plus most of July and August. Outside the high season, many midrange and top-end establishments in tourist destinations cut their room prices by 10% to 40%. They may also have special offers and low weekend rates. Budget accommodations are more likely to keep the same rates year-round. The hotels in the developed resort areas – like Cancún and Playa del Carmen – tend to publish their rates in US dollars, meaning a flux in the peso-to-dollar exchange rate can mean a big swing in actual on-the-ground prices. In the rest of the peninsula, most places stick with the peso, sometimes moving their prices to follow the swings of the almighty greenback.

For peak times at popular destinations, it's best to reserve a room in advance and you'll generally save a bundle by reserving over the internet.

Accommodations prices are subject to two taxes: *impuesto de valor agregado* (IVA, the value-added tax; 15%) and *impuesto sobre hospedaje* (ISH, the lodging tax; 2% in most states). Many budget and some mid-range establishments only charge these taxes if you require a receipt. Generally, though, IVA and ISH are included in quoted prices. In top-end hotels a price may often be given as, say, 'M$1000 *más impuestos*' (M$1000 plus taxes), in which case you must add 17% to the figure. When in doubt, you can ask '*¿Están incluidos los impuestos?*' (Are taxes included?).

WEB RESOURCES

Tourist offices and advertisements in local newspapers (especially English-language newspapers) are good sources of information on local house rentals, as are www.locogringo.com and www.tacolist.com.mx. Budget travelers will want to check out the deals on places like **HostelWorld** (www.hostelworld.com) and **Hostelling International Mexico** (www.hostellingmexico.com). For top-end accommodation, you're best off looking at the major aggregators, such as www.expedia.com, www.travelocity.com, www.orbitz.com, www.hotels.com and www.priceline.com.

>DIVING & SNORKELING

Without a doubt, diving and snorkeling are the area's top activity draw. The Caribbean is world famous for its wonderful coral reefs and translucent waters full of tropical fish and the Mesoamerican reef – which stretches all the way from Isla Contoy in the north to the crystal-clear waters of Belize in the south – is the second-largest barrier reef in the world.

The first stop on any diver's trip here should be to Cozumel (p78), where you can enjoy drift dives, wreck dives, cave dives and shallow-water snorkels all in one week.

And though Cozumel is a must-see, serious divers will be happy to know that there are great dives to be enjoyed all along the eastern coast of the Yucatán Peninsula. Cancún (p36), Isla Mujeres (p56), Puerto Morelos (p52), Playa del Carmen (p66) and Xcalak (p105) are all prime places to kick off a diving vacation. Just off the Costa Maya, the Banco Chinchorro, the largest coral atoll in the northern hemisphere, was hard-hit by Hurricane Dean in 2007, but is, according to local divers, recovering well.

Most of the places listed above are also great snorkeling spots. The best snorkeling is generally reached by boats, but the areas near Akumal (p77), Isla Mujeres (p56) and Cozumel (pictured right, p84) all offer pretty decent beach-accessed spots.

In the unlikely event that you find yourself yawning at the green morays, eagle rays, dolphins, sea turtles, nurse sharks and multitudinous tropical fish, you're ready to dive a cenote (a deep limestone sinkhole containing water). Hook up with a reputable dive shop and prepare for (in the immortal words of Monty Python) 'something completely different.'

You'll be lucky if you see four fish on a typical cenote dive. Trade brilliance for darkness and blue for black, check that your regulator is working flawlessly and enter a world unlike anything you've ever dived before. Soar around stalactites and stalagmites, hover above cake-frosting formations and glide around in tunnels that will make you think you're in outer space.

Keep in mind that these are fragile environments. Avoid applying sunscreen or insect repellent right before entering. Use care when approaching, entering or exiting, as the rocks are often slippery. Loud noises such as yelling disturb bats and other creatures – though most people find themselves subdued by their presence in these caverns. In rare cases, tourists have been seriously injured or killed by climbing on the roots or stalactites.

The best cenote dives are located just outside Puerto Morelos (p52), Tulum (p92) and Playa del Carmen (p71).

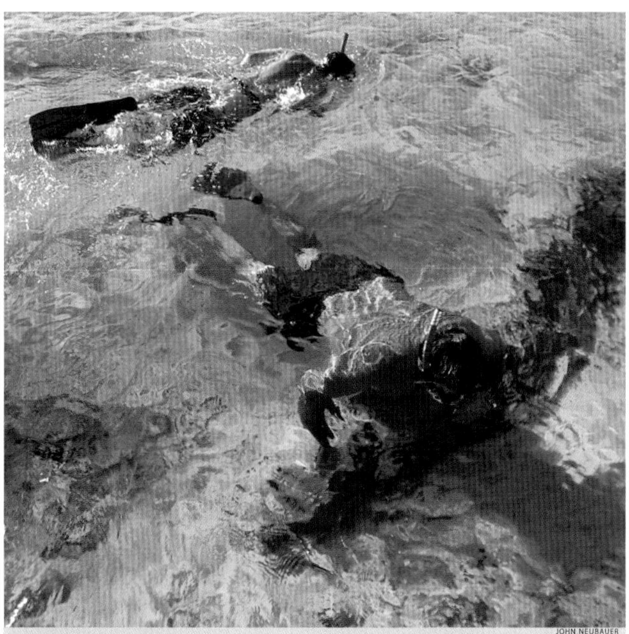

JOHN NEUBAUER

BEST CENOTES

- Cenote Dos Ojos (p77)
- Gran Cenote (p94)
- Cenote Angelita (p92)
- Cristalino Cenote (p71)
- Cuzamá (p116)

BEST DIVES

- Palancar Gardens (p88)
- Santa Rosa Wall (p88)
- Barracuda (p60)
- 40 Cannons (p104)
- Punta Sur (p88)

>FOOD

The Yucatán's rich cultural tapestry extends well beyond the traditional markets and favorite Tex-Mex dishes many of us have come to love. Gastronomic explorers will find a wealth of new, interesting and exotic foods to try as they move from the coast with its seafood-heavy menus on into the countryside, where traditional dishes, such as *cochinita pibil* (slow-cooked pork) and brash *recados* (locally blended spices or marinades that add a zing to any dish), rule supreme.

Nearly everybody has a preconceived notion of what Mexican food should taste like – rice, beans, tortillas, chili peppers, salsas, spicy seared meats, lime, salt...your basic taco or enchilada – but leave your expectations at the door, because the regional cuisine of the Yucatán is far more varied and delicate than just that.

Of course, this being Mexico's largest tourist destination, there's plenty of international fare up for grabs. The restaurants in Cancún's Zona Hotelera tend to be large chain affairs, though there are a few standouts worth checking out, while the in-the-know crowd often heads downtown for cheaper eats and a slightly more authentic setting.

Serious gourmands will want to head to Playa del Carmen, stroll down Quinta Av and pick a scene that fits their tastes – there's raucous bar-and-grills, sophisticated eateries featuring modern takes on traditional

BEST SEAFOOD

- Lorenzillo's (p41)
- Los de Pescado (p50)
- Costa Brava (p83)
- La Cocay (p85)
- Leaky Palapa (p107)

BEST MEXICAN FARE

- La Res Cortés (p49)
- Parque Las Palapas (p50)
- La Guacamaya (p76)
- El Mariachi (p97)
- 100% Agave (p104)

BEST VALUE

- Mañana (p61)
- Mercado 28 (p47)
- Señor Tacombi (p76)
- Cocina Económica Las Palmas (p83)
- Salsalito Taco Shop (p97)

BEST SPOT FOR ROMANCE

- Mocambo (p42)
- La Dolce Vita (p41)
- Sunset Grill (p64)
- John Gray's Place (p74)
- Posada Margherita (p97)

DAVID PEEVERS

Mexican favorites, plus a large selection of international choices (Italian, Asian, Argentinean…you name it).

Some of the best food along the coast can be had at the small *puestos* (market stands) and family restaurants. As always, have a look around to assess the general cleanliness of the place. A good tip: if there's a lot of locals there, it's likely to be clean and delicious.

Desayuno (breakfast) is usually served in restaurants and cafeterias from 8:30am to 11am and it tends to be on the heavy side. In Mexico the main meal is *comida* (lunch). It's usually served from 2pm to 4:30pm in homes, restaurants and cafes. *Cena* (dinner) is served anytime after 7pm. Restaurants in small towns won't remain open beyond 8:30pm or 9pm.

>KIDS

Snorkeling in caves, playing on the beach, hiking in the jungle...kids will find plenty of ways to keep busy in the Yucatán. And as elsewhere in Mexico, children take center stage – with few exceptions, children are welcome at all kinds of hotels and in virtually every cafe and restaurant. In this book you'll find especially child-friendly places identified with the icon.

Apart from the ruins, beaches and swimming pools, you'll find excellent special attractions, such as amusement parks, water parks, zoos, aquariums and other fun places, on the peninsula.

Kids can also enjoy activities such as snorkeling, riding bicycles, boating and watching wildlife. Archaeological sites are a fun way to introduce history into your vacation and are great spots for children to play and explore.

Zip-lining has become popular in recent years and many of the cenote adventures also offer (or include) this adrenaline-filled, bird's-eye dangle over the jungle canopy. It's not as heart-stopping as bungee jumping or parachuting, but it's a whole lot safer and still pretty good fun. Most of the ecoparks in Quintana Roo (p69) also offer rides, as do many of the tour operators out of Cancún and Playa del Carmen.

With its large resort hotels – many of which have their own kids clubs, plus pools, organized activities and game rooms – Cancún is probably the easiest spot for families. It's close to the airport and it's an easy launching point for day trips (p43) to the ruins at Chichén Itzá (p110), the turtle farm on Isla Mujeres (p58) or the slew of snorkeling spots nearby (p39).

Both Isla Mujeres and Cozumel offer up a variety of kid-friendly adventures, from the excellent swimming at the beach at Isla Mujeres'

BEST KODAK MOMENTS

- > Xcaret (pictured right, p69)
- > Cobá (p96)
- > Parque Chankanaab (p84)
- > Punta Laguna (p94)
- > Chichén Itzá (p110)

BEST LEARNING EXPERIENCES

- > Isla Mujeres Turtle Farm (p58)
- > Tulum (p90)
- > Mérida (p115)
- > Nuevo Durango (p43)
- > Ruta de los Conventos (p107)

GREG JOHNSTON

Hotel Garrafón de Castilla (p60) to animal shows at Cozumel's Parque Chankanaab (p84). The Jardín Botánico Yaax Che (p52) and cenotes (p52) near Puerto Morelos are also fun, as are the string of cenotes and natural lagoons found south of Playa del Carmen (p71). A trip all the way down to Tulum (p90) may be a little bit much for young ones, but older kids will love exploring the beach-front ruins and romping on the shore.

It's always fun to introduce a bit of culture into your trip and an excursion into the Mayan countryside to places like Nuevo Durango (p43), Punta Laguna (p94) or Izamal (p113) can be an eye-opening and life-changing experience for every member of your family.

>NATURE RESERVES

The Yucatán's amazing biological preserves offer hikers, kayakers and other outdoor wanderers the chance to spot birds and animals few people still see in the wild. Even the quickest of detours brings you face to face with things you thought you'd only see on TV, or you can invest a bit more time for a once-in-a-lifetime multiday trek or kayak.

Mexico's largest wildlife reserve, the Reserva de la Biosfera Calakmul (p118), offers up your best chance of seeing a jaguar or howler monkey – plus you'll get to explore a Maya ruin not often visited by tourists. That said, an expedition here takes at least two or three days, especially if you are leaving from Cancún. But it is definitely worth it, especially for bird lovers, who will have the chance of seeing some 230 different kinds of birds, of which most are resident species, including the ocellated turkey, a large bird with rainbow plumage like a peacock.

Similar wildlife-watching experiences can be had on a two-day trip to Río Lagartos (p112) on the Gulf coast. Birders and nature lovers staying on Isla Mujeres will want to take a day trip out to Isla Contoy (p64), while those in Tulum shouldn't miss the vast estuaries of the Sian Ka'an Biosphere Reserve (p98), where you may also spot manatees. If you find yourself on the Costa Maya, you'll want to rent a kayak to explore the estuaries near Xcalak (p106) or head out for the day to explore the azure waters of Laguna Bacalar (p107).

For adventure at your fingertips, head to Punta Laguna (p94), an easy enough day trip from the resort areas around Tulum, Cancún and Playa

BEST SPOTS FOR BIRDERS

- > Isla Contoy (p64)
- > Río Lagartos (p112)
- > Calakmul (p118)

BEST CHANCE OF SEEING A MONKEY…OR MAYBE A JAGUAR

- > Calakmul (p118)
- > Punta Laguna (p94)
- > Jardín Botánico Yaax Che (p52)

BEST SPOTS TO SEE NESTING TURTLES

- > Akumal (p77)
- > Isla Mujeres Turtle Farm (pictured right, p58)
- > Xcacel-Xcacelito (p77)

BEST CHANCE OF GETTING LOST

- > Sian Ka'an Biosphere Reserve (p98)
- > Laguna Bacalar (p107)
- > Calakmul (p118)

DAVID PEEVERS

del Carmen. Here, native guides take you on a walking tour that will most probably include sightings of spider and howler monkeys. Extended trips may be possible, too, but should only be undertaken by expert trekkers who have ample experience.

Yucatán also offers DIY-style hikes just about anywhere you feel like parking the car. Ruined haciendas, overgrown jungle trails, a mile of flotsam-studded coastline – the wonders of Yucatán's outdoors are limited mainly by your own imagination and what you have time for.

>RUINS

A trip to Cancún and the Riviera Maya would really be incomplete without at least one excursion to a Maya ruin. While a journey to an archaeological site like Chichén Itzá or Cobá will feed your intellect, it's important to keep in mind that, in the Yucatán, history is not confined to the past. It ebbs and flows through every aspect of modern life, like a thousand-limbed juggernaut hell-bent on its own preservation.

You'll notice it in the sun-seared faces of the *huipil*-clad *mestiza* women as they bring their wares to market, in the 'secret' language of your waiter – who just might have grown up speaking Maya, not Spanish, and is now learning English – and in the rich cultural patrimony that

BEST INDIANA JONES EXPERIENCES

> Calakmul (p118)
> Cobá (pictured below, p96)
> Ruta Puuc (p116)
> Dzibanché (p107)
> Río Bec (p118)

BEST SPOTS TO PRACTICE SPEAKING MAYA

> Solferino (p117)
> Punta Laguna (p94)
> Ruta de los Conventos (p107)
> Mérida (p115)
> Felipe Carrillo Puerto (p103)

JOHN NEUBAUER

JOHN ELK III

ripples through every aspect of daily life for the people of the peninsula. All one need do to witness the currents of modern life is step two blocks away from the tourist zone, where colorful markets, out-of-sight taco stands and otherworldly sights, sounds and smells await.

To step further back into history – to the days of the Maya kings, bloodletting, sun worship and ball games that ended in sacrifice – a trip to the Maya-Toltec site of Chichén Itzá (pictured above, p110) is probably the first on your list. Recently named one of the New Seven Wonders of the World, this site is quite impressive, though many complain that it's overcrowded and wish they could ascend the pyramids. Lucky for those glass-half-empty types, there are plenty of less-visited ruins out there, including the remote towering pyramids of Calakmul (p118) – stop at Dzibanché and Kohunlich on your way (p107) – and the low-slung arcades and arches found along the Ruta Puuc (p116). Kids love exploring the seafront ruins at Tulum (p92), while history buffs will appreciate the rich historic context of the jungle-shrouded ruins at Cobá (p96). Beyond these mainstays, there's plenty of smaller sites to explore in Cozumel (p84) and even in Cancún proper (p38).

>NIGHTLIFE

Cancún is one of the biggest spring-break destinations for US college students with good reason. The large discos of the resort's Zona Hotelera (p43) offer spectacular floor shows, scantily clad waitstaff, nightly drink specials and loud music. The downtown area has a few lower-key bars, Roots (p51) being a perennial favorite.

In Isla Mujeres, the Poc-Na Hostel (p65) has a great beachfront bonfire-of-the-hippies bar that's open to one and all and there are a handful of fun bars with live music along the Hidalgo pedestrian mall.

Playa del Carmen (p76) is the best nightlife scene on the coast: peaced-out lounges, beachfront music and dance joints, and more firm and toned skin per square inch than anywhere else in the Riviera Maya. The party here is always good...sometimes even too good, especially for those hoping to take an excursion the next day.

The party scene in other smaller resorts of the area – Tulum, Cozumel, Holbox, Puerto Morelos and the other small towns of the Riviera Maya – is surprisingly subdued. Most places close early (around midnight, or when people start to leave) and you're more likely to just chill out with fellow travelers than dance till dawn with strangers.

There's something for nearly every taste and style, making for nonstop fun. And in Mexico, there's always time for one more tequila.

BEST CHANCES OF HOOKING UP

> Dady'O (p44)
> Blue Parrot Bar (p77)
> Poc-Na Hostel (p65)
> Karamba (p51)
> Playa 69 (p77)

BEST LIVE MUSIC

> Roots (p51)
> Fusion (pictured right, p76)
> Sabor Latino (p52)
> Fayne's (p65)
> Don Pepe's (p55)

FUSION BAR

>WATER SPORTS

For those who like to keep their head above water, there are still plenty of water-bound activities – kayaking, fishing and kiteboarding, to name a few – to keep you busy. Yucatán's coastal lagoons and sheltered bays make for magnificent kayaking and there's often interesting wildlife to be seen among the mangrove thickets. It's uncommon to see manatees (unheard of now in the Cancún area) but possible in the protected reserves near Tulum (p98) and Xcalak (p105).

Kayaking tours in northern Quintana Roo can be booked through Playa del Carmen's Alltournative (p68). In the south, book tours through Community Tours Sian Ka'an (p93).

You can rent equipment in Cancún or Isla Holbox for DIY adventures all along the Caribbean coast. You can also get out onto the water at Rancho Punta Venado (p77), Tankah (p77) and Xcalak (p105). The Laguna Bacalar (p107) offers some freshwater adventure opportunities.

The same winds that can make a dive challenging or even cause it to be canceled are a kitesurfer's dream. Strong northeast winds make Isla Holbox (p116) a prime spot for kiteboarding, though there are currently no guide or rental outfits on the island. Cancún (p39) and Tulum (p92) both have companies offering kiteboarding lessons.

If surfing is your thing, then you're in the wrong spot, buddy. But the windward side of Cozumel does offer a few waves bigger than what you'd see in a toilet bowl. And Cancún gets a few rollers in *norte* season (November to February).

The Caribbean coast has some good sport fishing and the areas around the Sian Ka'an Biosphere Reserve (p98) and Xcalak (p105) are famous for their catch-and-release fly-fishing. Further north, fishing can be done on Isla Mujeres and around Cozumel. In Yucatán state, Río Lagartos (p112) is a popular spot.

>BEACHES

The Quintana Roo coast offers up some of the best beaches in the world. We know it's a bold statement, but heaven help us if it isn't true. While Cancún's series of beaches (p39) are largely artificial, they are some of the most beautiful on the coast. This said, you'll be sharing them with a fair number of hawkers and lobster-red tourists.

Those seeking a bit of reprieve should consider the shallow waters between Isla Mujeres' Playa Norte (p58) and Punta Norte. A perfect spot for low-key, no-current splashing and wading, this is a great place for anyone with kids in tow. The murky Gulf-coast waters surrounding Isla Holbox (p116) are less desirable for swimming, but the beach is generally deserted, making for ideal sunset strolls.

The beach scene gets even better as you head southward from Cancún: less people means more space for you and your crew. Puerto Morelos' beaches (p52) are a sweet honey brown, as are the see-and-be-seen spots near Playa del Carmen (p68), where G-strings are in (for both men and women) and tops are only worn come dinner time. The beaches across the way in Cozumel (p80) aren't great for sunning, but there are several beachfront lagoons (p84) ideal for snorkeling and swimming.

Heading south from Playa, you pass a series of wonderful laid-back spots (p77) – Paamul, Rancho Punta Venado, Akumal, Xcacel-Xcacelito and Tankah – as well as a few ecoparks (p69) that offer amazing lagoons, fun activities for the kids and jaw-dropping oceanfront views.

Continuing south, you have Tulum's grainy-white beach (p92) – it comes complete with its own Maya ruin – and the forgotten shores of the Sian Ka'an Biosphere Reserve (p98), plus the satiny aqua-blue waters of the Costa Maya (p102).

BEST SPOT FOR A ROMANTIC BEACHFRONT WALK

> Tulum (p92)
> Isla Mujeres (p58)
> Playa del Carmen (p68)
> Rancho Punta Venado (p77)
> Puerto Morelos (p52)

BEST CHANCE OF HAVING THE BEACH TO YOURSELF

> Mahahual (p102)
> Sian Ka'an Biosphere Reserve (p98)
> Xcacel-Xcacelito (p77)
> Tankah (p77)
> Isla Holbox (p116)

>BACKGROUND

GUYLAIN DOYLE

Souvenirs depicting Mayan figures at Chichén Itzá (p140)

HISTORY

The Maya – accomplished astronomers and mathematicians, and architects of some of the grandest monuments ever known – created their first settlements in what is now Guatemala as early as 2400 BC. Over the centuries the expansion of Maya civilization moved steadily northward and by AD 550 great Maya city-states were established in southern Yucatán. In the 10th century, with the invasion of the bellicose Toltecs from Central Mexico, the great cities of southern Yucatán slowly dissolved as attention shifted northward to new power centers like Chichén Itzá.

The last of the great Maya capitals, Mayapán, started to collapse around 1440, when the Xiu Maya and the Cocom Maya began a violent and protracted struggle for power. In 1540 Spanish conquistador Francisco de Montejo the Younger (son of legendary conquistador Francisco de Montejo the Elder) utilized the tensions between the still-feuding Maya sects to conquer the area. The Spaniards allied themselves with the Xiu against the Cocom, finally defeating the Cocom and gaining the Xiu as reluctant converts to Christianity.

Montejo the Younger, along with his father and cousin (named, you guessed it, Francisco de Montejo), founded Mérida in 1542 and within four years brought most of the Yucatán Peninsula under Spanish rule. The Spaniards divided up the Maya lands into large estates, where the natives were put to work as indentured servants.

When Mexico won its independence from Spain in 1821, the new Mexican government used the Yucatecan territory to create huge plantations for the cultivation of tobacco, sugarcane and *henequén* (agave rope fiber). The Maya, though legally free, were enslaved in debt peonage to the rich landowners.

In 1847, after being oppressed for nearly 300 years by the Spanish and their descendants, the Maya rose up in a massive revolt. This was the beginning of the War of the Castes. Finally, in 1901, after more than 50 years of sporadic but often intense violence, a tentative peace was reached; however, it would be another 30 years before the territory of Quintana Roo came under official government control. To this day some Maya do not recognize that sovereignty.

The commercial success of Cancún in the early 1970s led to hundreds of miles of beachfront property along the Caribbean coast being sold off to commercial developers, displacing many small fishing communities. While many indigenous people still eke out a living by subsistence agriculture or fishing, large numbers now work in the construction and service industries. Some individuals and communities, often with outside encouragement, are having a go at ecotourism, opening their lands to tourists or serving as guides.

LIFE AS A YUCATECAN

Culture is an ever-evolving monster and the regional identity of the Yucatán is arguably changing faster today than ever before. The erosion of Maya culture, migration to large cities and tourist centers, and the ever-pervasive influence of Mexico's neighbors to the north are morphing and distorting the cultural zeitgeist, creating a new paradigm for a region with a growing identity crisis.

Travelers often comment on the open, gentle and gregarious nature of the people of the Yucatán, especially the Yucatecan Maya. Here more than elsewhere in Mexico, it seems, you find a willingness to converse and a genuine interest in outsiders. This openness is all the more remarkable when you consider that the people of the Yucatán Peninsula have fended off domination by outsiders for so long – a situation that persists today. The best land is owned or purchased by gringos, Chilangos (natives of Mexico City) or criollos (people of Spanish descent) and, with few exceptions, those filling the desirable jobs and making infrastructure decisions are not Maya.

And with the tourist industry fast becoming the kingmaker in the region, Maya culture seems to evaporate faster and faster as the Maya people abandon their language and traditions (highly rooted in an agrarian way of life) and head to Cancún or Playa del Carmen to work as busboys and waiters, maids and construction workers. But survival has always been at a premium here and the Maya (and the rest of the region's poor) are finding ways to survive, be it by moving to the US to find employment or working in the *maquiladoras* (export-only factories paying workers from around M$54 per day) in Mérida during the week, only making it home to family (the true heart and soul of Mexican culture) on the weekends. This increased isolation from the essential and fundamental Mexican element, *la familia* (the family), is leading to increases in modern-day ailments like the dreaded 'Ds': divorce and depression.

But beyond this distinct history and the modern-day challenges facing the region, the people of the Yucatán share many cultural traits with other Mexicans. That is to say, despite the winds of progress and modernization, many of the age-old traditions still remain. Like their compatriots in Oaxaca, Chihuahua or Mexico City, they highly value family bonds and are only truly themselves within the context of the family. Though they are hardworking, the people of the region still like to enjoy leisure pursuits to the fullest and there's never a shortage of fiestas and fun. Yucatecans are also deeply religious, though their faith is a mélange of pre-Hispanic beliefs and Catholicism. As elsewhere in Mexico, traditional gender roles may seem exaggerated to the outsider, though the level of machismo on the peninsula is somewhat less pronounced.

ARCHITECTURE

Maya architecture is amazing for its achievements but perhaps even more amazing for what it did not achieve. Maya architects never seem to have used the true arch (a rounded arch with a keystone) and never thought to put wheels on boxes for use as wagons to move the thousands of tons of construction materials needed in their tasks. They had no metal tools – they were technically a Stone Age culture – yet could build breathtaking temple complexes and align them so precisely that windows and doors were used as celestial observatories with great accuracy.

The arch used in most Maya buildings is the corbeled arch (or, when used for an entire room rather than a doorway, corbeled vault). In this technique, large flat stones on either side of the opening are set progressively inward as they rise. The two sides nearly meet at the top and this 'arch' is then topped by capstones. Though they served the purpose, the corbeled arches severely limited the amount of open space beneath them. In effect, Maya architects were limited to long, narrow vaulted rooms.

The Maya also lacked draft animals (horses, donkeys, mules or oxen). All the work had to be done by humans, on their feet, with their arms and backs, without wagons or even wheelbarrows.

ARTS

The Yucatán's arts and crafts scene is enormously rich and varied. The influence of the Maya or Spanish cultures (or both) appears in almost every facet of Yucatecan art, from their dance and music to the clothes and hats they wear.

PRE-HISPANIC ART

The Classic Maya, at their cultural height from about AD 300 to 900, were perhaps ancient Mexico's most artistic people. They left countless beautiful stone sculptures, of complicated design and meaning but possessing an easily appreciated delicacy of touch – a talent also expressed in their unique architecture. Subjects were typically rulers, deities and significant events.

LITERATURE

One of Yucatán's earliest known literary works is the *Chilam Balam*. Written in Maya after the conquest, it is a compendium of Maya history, prophecy and mythology collected by priests from the northern Yucatán town of Chumayel.

Diego de Landa, a Spanish friar, could be said to have produced the first literary work in Spanish from the Yucatán, *Relación de las Cosas de Yucatán* (An Account of the Things of Yucatán), in which he relates his perception of the Maya's ceremonial festivals, daily life and traditions, even as he engineered their eradication.

Aside from (unsuccessfully) seeking US intervention against the Maya during the War of the Castes, Justo Sierra O'Reilly is credited with writing what is possibly the first Mexican novel, *La Hija del Judio*. About the ill-fated romance of a Jewish merchant's daughter in colonial Mexico, this superior work of fiction was originally published during the 1840s as a series in Sierra's Campeche newspaper, *El Fénix,* and later republished in its entirety.

In more recent times, the Yucatecan author Emilio Abreu Gómez synthesized the peninsula's Maya heritage in fictional works, including the novel *Canek: History and Legend of a Maya Hero,* the story of an indigenous laborer's struggle against injustice.

Novelist, playwright and art critic Juan García Ponce, who died in 2003, is perhaps the Yucatán's best-known modern literary figure. *Imagen Primera* (First Image) and *La Noche* (The Night), collections of his short stories, make good starting points for exploring the Mérida-born writer's abundant output.

TRAVEL LITERATURE

Incidents of Travel in Central America, Chiapas & Yucatan and *Incidents of Travel in Yucatan,* by John L Stephens, are fascinating accounts of adventure and discovery by the enthusiastic 19th-century amateur archaeologist. Both books contain superb illustrations by architect Frederick Catherwood, who accompanied Stephens in 1839 and 1841 as he explored a large part of the Maya region.

Aldous Huxley traveled through Mexico, too; *Beyond the Mexique Bay,* first published in 1934, has interesting observations on the Maya. Also interesting is Graham Greene's *The Lawless Roads,* chronicling the writer's travels through Chiapas and Tabasco in 1938.

Time Among the Maya: Travels in Belize, Guatemala, and Mexico, by Ronald Wright, is a thoughtful account of numerous journeys made among the descendants of the ancient Maya and will certainly help you to get a feel for Maya culture as you travel the region.

Most of the Maya codices were destroyed during the conquest (only four exist today), but the *Chilam Balam,* written by a Maya prophet during the late 18th century, chronicles many of the oral traditions and legends of the Yucatec Maya. It's a rather obscure read, however, and you're better off checking out the Guatemalan Quiche Maya sacred text known as the *Popol Vuh*.

Michael Coe's *The Maya* is the definitive history text of the Maya people. *The Caste War of Yucatán,* by Nelson A Reed, chronicles the fascinating history of the war.

MUSIC

Two styles of music are traditionally associated with the Yucatán: the *jarana* and *trova yucateca,* both of which you will see performed (in some form or other) in the tourist areas of the Quintana Roo coast.

A type of festive dance music, the *jarana* is generally performed by a large ensemble consisting of two trumpets, two clarinets, one trombone, a tenor sax, timbales and a guiro (percussion instrument made from a grooved gourd). The music pauses for the singers to deliver *bombas* – ad-libbed verses, usually with a humorous double meaning, that are aimed at the object of their affections. A *jarana* orchestra always ends its performances with the traditional *torito,* a vivacious song that evokes the fervor of a bullfight.

A hybrid of Cuban, Spanish, Colombian and homegrown influences, the Yucatecan *trova* is a catchall term for romantic ballads, Cuban claves, tangos, boleros, Yucatecan folk songs and other tunes that can be strummed on a guitar by a *trovador* (troubador). The style is often played by the guitar trios who roam the squares of Mérida, seeking an audience to serenade.

(The usual serenade consists of five songs.) In any discussion of the *trova,* you're likely to hear the name Guty Cárdenas, nicknamed the 'Yucatecan nightingale.' Cárdenas only recorded for five years during the 1920s, but he's been remarkably influential. In a *trova,* as with *jaranas,* the subject matter is usually a suitor's paean of love to an unattainable sweetheart. March brings the Festival de Trova Yucateca to Mérida.

A more contemporary figure of Yucatecan song is Armando Manzanero, the singer and composer from Mérida. Though Manzanero speaks to an older generation, his songs are still being covered by contemporary pop stars like Luis Miguel and Alejandro Sanz. He is best known for heart-wrenching boleros, such as 'Adoro,' 'Te Extraño,' 'Contigo Aprendí' and 'Somos Novios' (a tune that English speakers are more likely to know as 'It's Impossible'), many of which have taken their place in the canon of Mexican standards.

DANCE

The Spanish influence on Maya culture is abundantly evident in the *jarana,* a dance Yucatecans have been performing for centuries. The dance bears more than a passing resemblance to the *jota,* performed in Spain's Alto Aragón region. The movements of the dancers, with their torsos held rigid and a formal distance separating men from women, are nearly identical; however, where the Spanish punctuate elegant turns of their wrists with clicks of their castanets, Maya women snap their fingers.

The best place to see dancers perform to the accompaniment of *jarana* is at *vaquerías* – homegrown fiestas held in the atriums of town halls or on haciendas. The women wear their best embroidered *huipiles,* flowers in their hair and white heels; men wear a simple, white cotton outfit with a red bandanna tucked into the waist. In Mérida, *vaquerías* are held weekly in the Plaza de Santa Lucía.

HANDICRAFTS

TEXTILES

Women throughout the Yucatán Peninsula traditionally wear straight, white cotton dresses called *huipiles,* the bodices of which are always embroidered. The tunic generally falls to just below the knee; on formal occasions it is worn with a lacy white underskirt that reaches the ankle. The *huipil* never has a belt, which would defeat its airy, cool design. Light, loose fitting and traditionally made of cotton (synthetics are occasionally used today), these garments are ideally suited for the tropics. Maya women have been wearing *huipiles* for centuries.

Also commonly worn on the peninsula (and similar to the *huipil* in appearance) is the *gala terno,* which is a straight, white, square-necked dress with an embroidered yoke and hem, worn over an underskirt that sports an embroidered strip near the bottom. It is fancier than a *huipil* and is often accompanied by a delicately hand-knitted shawl.

In addition to *huipiles, galas ternos* and shawls, Maya women throughout the peninsula are known for weaving lovely sashes, tablecloths and napkins.

WOODEN CRAFTS

In handicrafts shops across the peninsula, you'll come across beautiful wooden crafts, such as carved wooden panels and galleons.

The ancient Maya made wood carvings of their many gods, just as they carved the images of their deities in stone. The skill and techniques associated with this artistry survive to this day. The wooden panels are often a meter or more in height and feature a strange-looking character of unmistakably Maya imagination – the image will resemble figures you've seen at Maya ruins. If the carved image is one of a heavily adorned man raising a chalice, you're most likely looking at a representation of Itzamná, lord of the heavens; he's a popular figure on the wooden panels of contemporary Maya.

The Maya – so impressed with the Spanish galleons that arrived on their shores that they made meter-long models of the ships, complete with tiny sails – have been making wooden galleons for generations. Today the galleons that used to haul cargoes of hardwood back to Europe are gone, but the craft of galleon model making is alive and well in the Yucatán. Campeche is the state most associated with such items, but they are made by accomplished artisans in the states of Yucatán and Quintana Roo as well.

ENVIRONMENT

Large-scale tourism developments are affecting and sometimes erasing fragile ecosystems, especially along the Riviera Maya south of Cancún. Many hectares of vital mangrove swamp have been bulldozed and beaches where turtles once laid eggs are now occupied by resorts and condo-mondos. Major coastal developments have also played a role in the erosion of vital beach habitats, as was made evident when 2005's Hurricane Wilma swept away the very beaches and hotels that attract hordes of tourists annually to Cancún. For more information on environmental issues facing Cancún see p38.

With the proliferation of new hotels comes the need for freshwater sources, increasing the danger of salinization of the water table, as more and more water is pulled from natural aquifers. As employment seekers converge on Quintana Roo's tourist zones, demand for building materials to construct makeshift housing for the burgeoning population is also a persistent issue.

>DIRECTORY

TRANSPORTATION

ARRIVAL & DEPARTURE

AIR

The majority of flights into the peninsula arrive at busy **Cancún International Airport** (Aeropuerto Internacional de Cancún, CUN; ☎ 998-886-00-47; www.cancun-airport.com). The region's other gateways are **Cozumel airport** (CZM; ☎ 987-872-20-81; www.asur.com.mx), **Chetumal** (CTM; ☎ 983-832-08-98) and **Mérida** (MID; ☎ 999-946-15-30; www.asur.com.mx).

Airlines Flying to/from the Yucatán

Aeroméxico (code AM; ☎ 800-021-40-10; www.aeromexico.com; hub Mexico City) Campeche (☎ 981-823-40-44); Cancún (☎ 998-287-18-60); Mérida (☎ 999-920-12-93)

Air Berlin (code AB; ☎ in Germany 01-805-73-78-00; www.airberlin.com; hub Düsseldorf)

Alaska Airlines (code AS; ☎ 800-252-75-22; www.alaskaair.com; hub Seattle)

America West (code HP; ☎ 800-428-43-22; www.americawest.com; hub Phoenix)

American Airlines (code AA; ☎ 800-904-60-00; www.aa.com; hub Dallas) Cancún (☎ 998-866-00-86)

Continental Airlines (code CO; ☎ 800-900-50-00; www.continental.com; hub Houston) Cancún (☎ 998-866-00-06)

Copa (☎ 998-886-06-52; www.copaair.com)

Cubana (code CU; ☎ 52-5250-6355; www.cubana.co.cu; hub Havana) Cancún (☎ 998-887-72-10)

Delta Airlines (code DL; ☎ 800-123-47-10; www.delta.com; hub Atlanta) Cancún (☎ 998-866-06-60)

Frontier Airlines (code F9; ☎ in the USA 800-432-1359; www.frontierairlines.com; hub Denver)

Mexicana de Aviación (code MX; ☎ 800-801-20-10; www.mexicana.com; hub Mexico City) Cancún (☎ 998-881-90-90)

Northwest (code NW; ☎ 800-907-47-00) Cancún (☎ 998-866-00-44)

TACA Airlines (code TA; ☎ 800-400-82-22; www.taca.com; hub San Salvador) Cancún (☎ 998-866-00-08)

US Airways (code US; ☎ 800-428-43-22; www.usairways.com; hub Philadelphia)

Cancún International Airport

ADO (☎ 800-802-80-00; www.ado.com.mx) has a ticket booth in the airport (just after you pass customs), where you can buy cheap tickets to downtown Cancún (M$42) and to Playa del Carmen (M$106). Going to the airport from Ciudad Cancún, catch the same bus out of the main bus terminal.

Grayline Express Colectivos (M$195) depart for the Zona Hotelera and downtown from in front of the international terminal every 15 minutes.

DEPARTURE TAX

A departure tax equivalent to about US$48 is levied on international flights from Mexico. It's usually included in the price of your ticket, but if it isn't, you must pay in cash during airport check-in. Ask your travel agent in advance.

CLIMATE CHANGE & TRAVEL

Every form of transport that relies on carbon-based fuel generates CO_2, the main cause of human-induced climate change. Modern travel is dependent on aeroplanes and while they might use less fuel per kilometre per person than most cars, they travel much greater distances. It's not just CO_2 emissions from aircraft that are the problem. The altitude at which aircraft emit gases (including CO_2) and particles contributes significantly to their total climate change impact. The Intergovernmental Panel on Climate Change believes aviation is responsible for 4.9% of climate change – double the effect of its CO_2 emissions alone.

Lonely Planet regards travel as a global benefit. We encourage the use of more climate-friendly travel modes where possible and, together with other concerned partners across many industries, we support the carbon offset scheme run by ClimateCare. Websites such as climatecare.org use 'carbon calculators' that allow people to offset the greenhouse gases they are responsible for with contributions to portfolios of climate-friendly initiatives throughout the developing world. Lonely Planet offsets the carbon footprint of all staff and author travel.

Taxis into town or to the Zona Hotelera cost up to M$450 (up to four people) if you catch them right outside the airport. However, if you follow the access road out of the airport and past the traffic-monitoring booth (a total of about 1000ft), you can often flag down an empty taxi leaving the airport that will take you for much less (you can try for M$80 to M$100).

Colectivos head to the airport from a stand in front of the Hotel Cancún Handall on Av Tulum about a block south of Av Cobá. They charge M$25 per person and leave when full. The official rate for private taxis from the town center to the airport is M$150.

VISA

All international travelers – including Canadian and US nationals – will need a valid passport to enter the country, whether they enter by land, air or sea.

Every tourist must also have an easily obtainable Mexican government tourist card, which you are issued upon entry. Some nationalities also need to obtain visas. Because the regulations sometimes change, it's wise to confirm them with a Mexican embassy or consulate before you go. **Lonely Planet** (www.lonelyplanet.com) has links to updated visa information.

Citizens of the USA, Canada, EU countries, Australia, New Zealand, Iceland, Israel, Japan, Norway and Switzerland are among those who do not require visas to enter Mexico as tourists. The list changes from time to time; check well ahead of travel. Visa procedures, for those who need them, can take several weeks and you may be required to apply in your country of residence or citizenship.

GETTING AROUND

Getting around the Yucatán is a snap. The buses are good and the road between Cancún and Tulum is a major four-lane highway.

AIR

In addition to Aeroméxico and Mexicana de Aviación, each of the following has domestic flights within the Yucatán.

AeroCosta (☎ 998-884-03-83; aerocosta2001@cancuntips.com.mx)

Magnicharters (☎ 998-884-06-00; www.magnicharters.com.mx; Av Náder 93, Cancún)

BOAT

Ferries run from the mainland to Isla Mujeres (p58), Cozumel (p89) and Isla Holbox (p117).

BUS & COLECTIVO

UNO (☎ 800-702-80-00; www.uno.com.mx), **ADO GL** (☎ 800-702-80-00; www.adogl.com.mx) and **OCC** (☎ 800-822-23-69, www.occbus.com.mx) provide luxury services. **ADO** (☎ 800-802-80-00; www.ado.com.mx) sets the 1st-class standard.

Microbuses (micros) are small, fairly new, 2nd-class buses with about 25 seats, often running short routes between nearby towns. The biggest 2nd-class companies are Mayab, Oriente and **Noreste** (☎ 800-280-10-10; www.noreste.com.mx).

First-class buses typically cost around M$40 per hour of travel (45 to 50 miles). Deluxe buses may cost just 10% or 20% more than 1st class, or about 60% more for superdeluxe services such as UNO. Second-class buses cost 10% or 20% less than 1st class. Children under 13 pay half-price on many Mexican long-distance buses and, if they're small enough to sit on your lap, they will usually go for free.

Seats on deluxe and 1st-class lines such as UNO, ADO and OCC can be booked through **Ticketbus** (☎ 800-702-80-00; www.ticketbus.com.mx).

Colectivos are shared taxis or *microbuses,* usually servicing shorter distances.

CAR & MOTORCYCLE

Drivers should know some Spanish and have basic mechanical knowledge, reserves of patience and access to extra cash for emergencies. Auto rental in the Yucatán is expensive by US or European standards, but is not hard to organize. You'll save money by booking ahead of time over the internet.

Renters must provide a valid driver's license (your home license is OK), passport and major credit card, and are usually required to be at least 21 years old (sometimes 25 or, if you're aged 21 to 24, you may have to pay a surcharge). Read the small print of the rental agreement. In addition to the basic rental rate, you pay tax and insurance to the rental company and the full insurance that rental companies encourage can almost double the basic cost. You'll usually have the option of taking liability-only insurance at a lower rate, about M$130 per day. Ask exactly what the insurance options cover: theft and damage insurance may only cover a percentage of costs. It's best to have plenty of liability coverage: Mexican law permits the jailing of drivers after an accident until they have met their obligations to third parties. The complimentary car-rental insurance offered with some US credit cards does not always cover Mexico. Call your card company ahead of time.

Most rental agencies offer a choice between a per-kilometer deal or unlimited kilometers. Local firms may or may not be cheaper than the big international ones. In most places the cheapest car available (often a Volkswagen Beetle) costs M$250 to M$500 per day including unlimited kilometers, insurance and tax. If you rent by the week or month, the per-day cost can come down by 20% to 40%.

Motorcycles and scooters are available for rent in a few tourist centers. You're usually required to have a driver's license and credit card.

Some major firms in Mexico:

Alamo (☎ 800-849-80-01; www.alamo.com)
Avis (☎ 800-288-88-88; www.avis.com.mx)
Budget (☎ 800-700-17-00; www.budget.com.mx)
Europcar (☎ 800-201-20-84; www.europcar.com.mx)
Hertz (☎ 800-709-50-00; www.hertz.com)
National (☎ 800-716-66-25; www.nationalcar.com.mx)
Thrifty (☎ 55-5786-8268; www.thrifty.com.mx)

PRACTICALITIES

BUSINESS HOURS

The siesta tradition wisely lives on in this hot climate, with shops generally open from 9am to 2pm, then reopening from 4pm to 7pm Monday to Saturday. Some may not be open on Saturday afternoon. Shops in malls and coastal resort towns often open on Sunday. Supermarkets and department stores usually open from 9am or 10am to 10pm daily.

Government offices have similar hours to shops, only Monday to Friday and with greater likelihood of having the 2pm to 4pm lunch break. Tourism-related offices usually open on Saturday, too, from at least 9am to 1pm.

Banks are normally open 9am to 5pm Monday to Friday and some from 9am to 1pm Saturday. In smaller towns they may close earlier or not open on Saturday.

Casas de cambio (money-exchange offices) are usually open from 9am to 7pm daily, often with even longer hours in coastal resorts. Post offices typically open from 8am to 6pm Monday to Friday and 9am to 1pm Saturday.

Most museums have one closing day per week, typically Monday. On Sunday nearly all archaeological sites and museums offer free admission for Mexican nationals and the major ones can get very crowded.

In this book we only spell out opening hours where they do not fit the above parameters. See the Quick Reference inside the front cover for further typical opening hours.

DANGERS & ANNOYANCES

Despite often alarming media reports and official warnings for Mexico in general, the Yucatán Peninsula remains a safe place to travel and, with just a few precautions, you can minimize the risk of encountering problems.

Enjoy yourself in the ocean, but beware of undertows and riptides on any beach.

Women traveling alone, and even pairs of women, should be cautious about going to remote beach and jungle spots.

Cocaine and marijuana are prevalent in Mexico. The easiest way to avoid the problems related with these drugs is by avoiding them. If you get busted using or transporting illegal drugs, your consulate will not help you.

Foreign affairs departments can supply a variety of useful data about travel to Mexico:

Australia (☎ in Australia 02-6261-1111; www.dfat.gov.au)
Canada (☎ in Canada 800-267-8376, 613-944-4000; www.dfait-maeci.gc.ca)
UK (☎ in the UK 020-7008-1500; www.fco.gov.uk)
USA (☎ in the USA 888-407-4747; www.travel.state.gov)

HEALTH

Travelers to the Yucatán chiefly need to be careful about food- and water-borne diseases. Most of these illnesses are not life threatening, but they can certainly negatively impact your trip.

To prevent diarrhea, avoid tap water unless it has been boiled, filtered or chemically disinfected (eg by iodine tablets); only eat fresh fruits or vegetables if cooked or if you peel them; be wary of dairy products that might contain unpasteurized milk; and be very selective when eating food from street vendors.

Besides getting the proper vaccinations, it's important that you bring a good insect repellent. Bring medications in their original containers, clearly labeled.

A signed, dated letter from your physician describing all your medical conditions and medications, including generic names, is also a good idea. If carrying syringes or needles, be sure to have a physician's letter documenting their necessity.

INTERNET

For the laptop set, there's wi-fi in most midrange hotels. Not carrying a laptop? Worry not: there's an internet cafe on nearly every corner.

Campeche Travel (www.campeche.travel) Campeche State Tourism Board site.
Cancún Tips (www.cancuntips.com.mx) A good resource for mainstream entertainment in Cancún.
Loco Gringo (www.locogringo.com) A good site to book homes on the Riviera Maya.
Lonely Planet (www.lonelyplanet.com/mexico) Lonely Planet's Mexico portal.
Maya Yucatán (www.mayayucatan.com.mx) Yucatán State Tourism Board site.
Riviera Maya (www.rivieramaya.com) Has info on the Riviera Maya's sights and activities. There's also a handy calendar on the home page.
Taco List (www.tacolist.com.mx) Mexico's answer to craigslist.org.
Ticket Bus (www.ticketbus.com.mx) Check bus schedules and book tickets at this one-stop shop.
Yucatán Today (www.yucatantoday.com) Online version of free monthly magazine covering Yucatán and Campeche states.

LANGUAGE

Yes.	*Sí.*
No.	*No.*
Please.	*Por favor.*
Thank you.	*Gracias.*
You're welcome.	*De nada.*
May I?	*Permiso?*
Excuse me.	*Disculpe.*
What's your name?	*¿Cómo se llama usted?* (pol)
How do I get to ...?	*¿Cómo llego a ...?*
Help!	*¡Socorro!*

MONEY

Midrange travelers can live well in most parts of the peninsula for M$800 to M$1500 per person per day. Two people can usually find a clean, comfortable room with private bathroom and fan or air-conditioning for M$500 to M$1000 and use the rest to pay for food (a full lunch or dinner in a typical decent restaurant costs around M$120 to M$200), admission fees, transport and incidentals. Budget travelers should allot M$300 to M$600 each per day for accommodations and two meals a day in cheap restaurants. Add in other costs (like contracting a guide or taking a snorkeling trip) and you'll spend more like M$600 to M$800.

Top-end hotels and resorts run a wide spectrum of prices, often charging upwards of M$2000 for a room. Restaurants in the same class can charge M$250 to M$500 per person and are largely targeted at the tourist trade. In most cases you're better off eating at locals' joints.

Mexico's currency is the peso, usually denoted by the 'M$' sign. Prices are quoted in Mexican pesos in this book. The peso is divided into 100 centavos. Coins come in denominations of 20 and 50 centavos and one, two, five and 10 pesos; notes, in 20, 50, 100, 200, 500 and 1000 pesos.

The most convenient form of money is a major international credit or debit card – preferably two if you've got them. Visa, MasterCard and American Express cards can be used to obtain cash easily from ATMs (*cajero automático* in Spanish) in Mexico, and are accepted for payment by most airlines, car-rental companies, travel agents, many upmarket hotels, and some restaurants and shops. Visa is the most universally accepted. Occasionally there's a surcharge for paying by card. You can exchange currency in banks or at *casas de cambio,* which are often single-window kiosks.

The value-added tax (IVA) is levied at 15% throughout Mexico, except in Quintana Roo, where it's 10%. By law the tax must be included in prices quoted to you and should not be added afterward. Signs in shops and notices on restaurant menus often state *'IVA incluido.'* Occasionally they state instead that IVA must be added to the quoted prices.

Hotel rooms are also subject to a lodging tax (ISH). Each Mexican state sets its own rate (Quintana Roo's ISH is 3%), but in most it's 2%.

TELEPHONE

Local calls are cheap; international calls can be expensive, but needn't be if you call from the right place at the right time. Mexico is well supplied with fairly easy-to-use public card phones. *Locutorios* and *casetas de teléfono* (call offices where an on-the-spot operator connects the call for you) are quite widespread and can be cheaper than card phones. Voice Over Internet Protocol (VOIP) calling, eg Skype, is available from many internet cafes and is a great money saver. A final option is to call from your hotel, but hotels charge what they like for this service; it's nearly always cheaper to go elsewhere. These days, many GSM cellular phones work in Mexico, though you'll pay a hefty rate (more than US$2 per minute) for the service.

If you do need to make a collect call *(una llamada por cobrar),* you can do so from card phones without a card. Call an operator at ☎ 020 for domestic calls or ☎ 090 for international calls.

Some phone (or calling) cards from other countries can be used for making phone calls from Mexico by dialing special access numbers:

AT&T (☎ 01-800-288-28-72, 001-800-462-42-40)

Bell Canada (☎ 01-800-123-02-00, 01-800-021-19-94)
BT Chargecard (☎ 01-800-123-02-44)
MCI (☎ 001-800-674-70-00)
Sprint (☎ 001-800-877-80-00)

COUNTRY & CITY CODES

To call a town or city in Mexico other than the one you're in, you need to dial the long-distance prefix (☎ 01), followed by the area code (two digits for Mexico City, Guadalajara and Monterrey; three digits for everywhere else) and then the local number. For example, to make a call from Cancún to Mérida, dial ☎ 01, then the Mérida area code ☎ 999, then the seven-digit local number. We've included the area codes in the telephone numbers in this book.

To make international calls, dial the international prefix ☎ 00, followed by the country code, area code and local number. For example, to call New York City, dial ☎ 00, then the US country code ☎ 1, the New York City area code ☎ 212, then the local number.

To call a number in Mexico from another country, dial your international access code, then the Mexico country code ☎ 52, then the area code and number.

USEFUL PHONE NUMBERS

Emergency (☎ 066)
Domestic long-distance access code (☎ 01)
Information (☎ 040)
International access code (☎ 00)
Mexico country code (☎ 52)
National tourist assistance/information (☎ 800-903-92-00, 55-5250-0123)

TIPPING

In general, employees of small, cheap restaurants don't expect much in the way of tips – though they like to receive them – while those in resorts frequented by foreigners (such as in Cancún and Cozumel) expect you to be lavish in your largesse. At the latter, tipping is up to US levels of 15% or 20%; elsewhere 10% is usually plenty. If you stay a few days in one place, you should leave up to 10% of your room costs for the people who have kept your room clean (assuming they have). A porter in a midrange hotel would be happy with M$10 per bag. Car-parking attendants expect a tip of M$3 to M$5; the same is standard for gas-station attendants. Baggers in supermarkets are usually tipped a peso or two.

TOURIST INFORMATION

Just about every town of interest to tourists in the Yucatán has a state or municipal tourist office. They are generally helpful with maps, brochures and questions, and often some staff members speak English.

You can call the Mexico City office of the national tourism ministry, **Sectur** (☎ 55-5250-0123/51, 800-903-92-00, in the USA & Canada 800-446-3942, 800-482-9832, in Europe 800-1111-2266; www.visitmexico.com), at any time – 24 hours a day, seven days a week – for information or help in English or Spanish.

Here are the contact details for the head tourism offices of each state covered in this book:

Campeche (☎ 981-811-92-29, 800-900-22-67; www.campeche.travel)

Quintana Roo (☎ 983-835-08-60; http://sedetur.qroo.gob.mx, in Spanish)

Yucatán (☎ 999-930-37-60; www.mayayucatan.com)

TRAVELERS WITH DISABILITIES

Lodgings on the Yucatán Peninsula are generally not disabled-friendly, though some hotels and restaurants (mostly towards the top end of the market) and some public buildings now provide wheelchair access. The absence of institutionalized facilities is largely compensated for, however, by Mexicans' accommodating attitudes toward others and special arrangements are gladly improvised.

Mobility is easiest in the major tourist resorts and the more expensive hotels. Bus transportation can be difficult; flying or taking a taxi is easier.

Mobility International USA (☎ in the USA 541-343-1284; www.miusa.org) advises travelers with disabilities on mobility issues. Its website includes international databases of exchange programs and disability organizations, with several Mexican organizations listed.

In the UK, **Radar** (☎ 020-7250-3222; www.radar.org.uk) is run by and for disabled people. Its excellent website has links to good travel-specific sites.

Two further sources for travelers with disabilities are **MossRehab ResourceNet** (www.mossresourcenet.org) and **Access-able Travel Source** (www.access-able.com).

>INDEX

See also separate subindexes for Do (p158), Drink (p159), Eat (p159), Play (p159) , See (p160) and Shop (p160).

000 map pages

DO

DRINK

EAT

PLAY

000 map pages